BROCHURES

© Copyright 2009
INDEX BOOK, SL
Consell de Cent 160 local 3
08015 Barcelona
Phone: +34 93 454 5547
Fax: +34 93 454 8438
E-mail: ib@indexbook.com
URL: www.indexbook.com

Author: www.mitodesign.com

The captions and artwork in this book are based on material supplied by the designers whose work is included. No part of this publication may be reproduced or transmitted in any form or by any means, electronic or mechanical, including photocopy, recording or any information storage and retrieval system, without permission in writing from the copyright owner(s).

Printed in China ISBN: 978-84-96774-97-1
While every effort has been made to ensure accuracy, neither Index Book nor the author under any circumstances accept responsibility for any errors or omissions.

Canada
United States
Mexico
Guatemala
Panama
Puerto Rico
Ecuador
Venezuela
Colombia
Bolivia
Peru
Paraguay
Brazil
Uruguay
Argentina
Chile

INTRODUCTION

Welcome to the second edition of "From North to South America". This time, it is all about brochures.

You will find folders, catalogs, brochures and all kinds of printed materials all of them very original and conceptual.

Most designers thought that the Internet would spell the end of printed material. However, today we find brochures that are even more original and are full of soul and contemporary style, proving the difference between real and digital materials.

Enjoy
Mito Design

CHAPTERS

009 CULTURE

063 DESIGN

133 ENTERTAINMENT

187 FOOD

FIRM 207

HEALTH 243

TECHNOLOGY 269

EXTRAS 285

"A brochure or pamphlet is a leaflet advertisement. Brochures may advertise locations, events, hotels, products, services, etc. They are usually succinct in language and eye-catching in design."

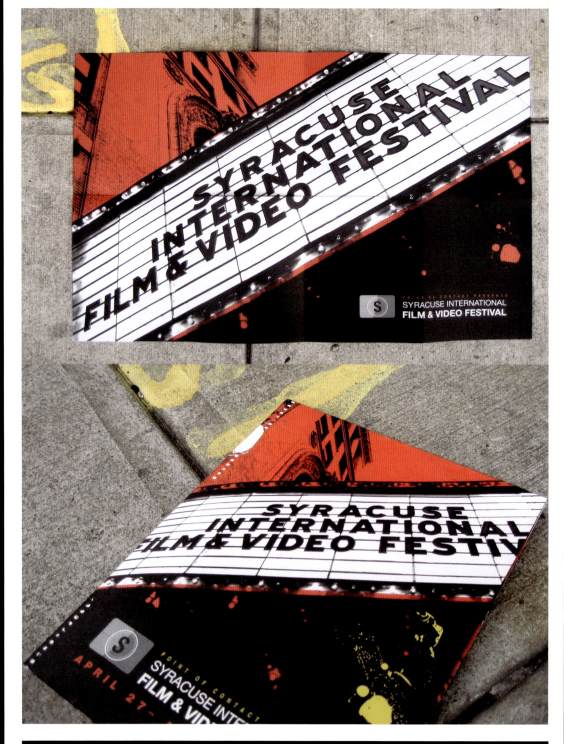

STUDIO
Hyperakt Design Group

CLIENT
Syracuse International

DESCRIPTION
Festival, events

STUDIO	_CLIENT_	_DESCRIPTION_
Hyperakt Design Group	Syracuse International	Film and video festival

STUDIO	_CLIENT_	_DESCRIPTION_
Hyperakt Design Group	Syracuse International	Film and video festival

STUDIO	_CLIENT_	_DESCRIPTION_
Gouthier Design	Saskia	Cultural documentation

STUDIO	_CLIENT_	_DESCRIPTION_
Gouthier Design	Saskia	Cultural documentation

STUDIO	_CLIENT_	_DESCRIPTION_
Ida Cheinman	Platts University	Art department presentation

STUDIO	_CLIENT_	_DESCRIPTION_
Ida Cheinman	Platts University	Art department presentation

PRINTMAKING

Plattsburgh State University printmaking program strives for an aesthetic balance between process and concept within a informal workshop environment. As an student in printmaking, you will explore various printmaking media, including intaglio, lithography, relief, letterpress and creative bookmaking. Both unique prints, and multiples are produced. While engaging in the creative study of printmaking, you will also investigate the history of the discipline and discuss related critical issues in contemporary art that will assist in your creativity.

10

PRINTMAKING STUDENTS ART WORK

Your visual experiences in Printmaking are supported by trips to museums in the area. Take a printmaking course, either as your art concentration area or simply as an art elective, and you'll be studying in a great facility.

PHOTOGRAPHY

The photography program at Plattsburgh State University offers you a complete spectrum of hands-on creative experiences that take you from the introductory to the advanced level. Advanced courses include black and white prints, color prints, color slides and the view camera. Our emphasis is on developing your individual expressive capabilities. There is a forum for exchanging ideas both in group and single session critiques. You will also learn the essentials of strong portfolio production and presentation, as well as being aware of the aesthetic concerns of other photographers.

9

PHOTOGRAPHY STUDENTS ART WORK

STUDIO	_CLIENT_	_DESCRIPTION_
Ida Cheinman	Platts University	Art department presentation

STUDIO	_CLIENT_	_DESCRIPTION_
Ida Cheinman	Platts University	Art department presentation

DESIGN STUDENTS ART WORK

PAINTING STUDENTS ART WORK

Graphic design at Plattsburgh State University is for the art major who wants to pursue a career in either print design or interactive media design. Our graphic design program gives you a focus in the visual communications field. You'll gain the expertise, ranging from creative problem-solving to the utilization of digital technology to assist in actualizing those ideas. To develop your design capabilities, you'll learn specific skills in concept thinking, typography, illustration, composition, and production design all emphasizing concise conceptual, aesthetic solutions. Since graphic design is all about enhancing communication, you'll learn how to best interpret and articulate marketing strategies.

The painting program at Plattsburgh State University will give you a course sequence designed to develop both your technical skills and personal artistic expression. In our beginning courses, students work from models, still lifes and landscapes, using both oil and acrylics. The emphasis here is on understanding color and space, on paint application and on composition. As an intermediate painting student, you'll explore various media and a wide range of painting issues, both past and present. When you reach the advanced painting levels, you will work more independently, refining your personal vision and skills as you prepare for a career as a painter. All beginning students have their own individual studio work areas. There are two additional studios to provide intermediate and advanced students with their personal and private, customized work environment.

7

8

GRAPHIC DESIGN

 PAINTING

Scholarships

The George and Nina Winkel Scholarship fund provides awards to students majoring in art or art history. Nina Winkel is recognized internationally as an outstanding sculptor and many of her works are housed in our permanent art collection. There are a number of other scholarships also available. However, scholarship applicants must apply and present a portfolio in order to be considered. Once you are accepted in our art program, you'll automatically receive scholarship information.

13

Art Museum

The Plattsburgh State Art Museum, Permanent Art Collection, and college-wide installations form a "museum without walls". The main areas are in the Myers Fine Arts Gallery, Myers Lobby, Winkel Sculpture Court and Rockwell Kent Gallery. These facilities produce over twenty-five historical and contemporary exhibitions a year, of both a national and regional nature. The Art Museum's permanent collection of over 1,800 items, offers a continual aesthetic resource for the visual arts student.

OUR VISITING ARTIST SERIES

Painters: Sigmund Abeles, Sue Coe, Linda Cros, Janet Fish, Audrey Flack, Gregory Gillespie, Sarah Gutwirth, Grace Hartigan, George Hofmann, Komar and Melamid Katherine Kadish, Lois Lane, Paul Matthews, Nancy Mladenoff, Alice Neel, Frank Owen, Phillip Pearlstein Joyce Rezendes, Miriam Schapiro Harriet Schorr, Joan Semmel, Nancy Spero, Jerome Witkin, **Sculptors:** Kim Abeles, Alice Aycock, Suzanne Bocanegra, Shaun Cassidy, William Childress, Hans Haacke, Duane Hanson, Basia Irland, Jon Isherwood Bill King, Susan Leopold, Marisol Dennis Oppenheim, Albert Paley Maura Sheehan, Charles Simonds, & Bonnie Baxter, **Book Artists:** Keiko Hara, Adele Henderson, Tracy Honn Katherine Kuehn, Ruth Lingen Frances Myers, Pati Scobey, Susan Share, Lisa Sweet, **Ceramists:** Garth Clark, William Daley, Michelle Gregor, Nicholas Kripal, Brook & Rose LeVan, Angelica Pozo, Betty Woodman **Photographers:** Lucinda Devlin Nathan Farb, Phyllis Galembo Amanda Means, Eric Landsberg Jolene Rickard, Meridel Rubenstein Ralph Steiner, Jerry Uelsmann **Video Artists:** Vito Acconci, Les Levine, Sherry Miller & Ralph Hockings, Adrian Piper, Bill Viola **Historians, Curators:** Lucy Lippard Thomas McEvilley, Robert Morgan Robert Rosenblum, Susan Sontag Leo Steinberg, Karen Wilkin, Robert Pincus Witten **Gallery Dealers:** Ivan Karp, Holly Solomon **Mixed Media Artists:** David Cabrera, Alan Magee Phyllis McGibbon, William Wegman **Graphic Designers:** James Victore Resa Blatman

ALL THE CULTURE OF A LARGE CITY WITHOUT THE SMOG AND ATTITUDE

Our Location

A great school is more than excellent facilities and large working studios. We have all that and more. Besides outstanding facilities and equipment, we have one of the most beautiful campuses around. And we don't just mean in New York State. Sure, some schools have floors and floors of work space (actually, so do we). But, at Plattsburgh State, we add to your cultural enrichment by being in the Adirondack Mountains and Champlain Valley regions, the most beautiful regions in New York State. The city of Plattsburgh, a small community of 43,000 residents, is noted for its clean, tree-lined streets, easygoing style of living, and its friendly, hospitable residents. Plattsburgh State University is easily accessible via scenic I-87. Cosmopolitan Montreal, Canada's largest city, is an hour away, as are Burlington, Vermont and Lake Placid, America's Olympic Village. When you visit our campus you'll know exactly what we mean about its beauty. There's art everywhere. Everywhere. Student art is tastefully mixed with the art of famous professionals in every building. Inside and throughout the grounds. It's like being in a living museum. Not only is it visually stimulating, it's tangible proof of the respect and support the visual arts are given by our college administration.

14

How to Apply

We, the art faculty, invite you to visit our campus for a personal interview and portfolio review. If you would like further information, please write or phone: Chairperson, Art Department, Myers Fine Arts Building, Plattsburgh State University, Plattsburgh, NY 12901, (518) 564-2179.

Plattsburgh State University, in recognition of its educational mission, its social concern, its responsibility for the personal development of individuals, and its concern for the rights of individuals, established a college policy of Equal Education and Employment Opportunity and Affirmative Action.

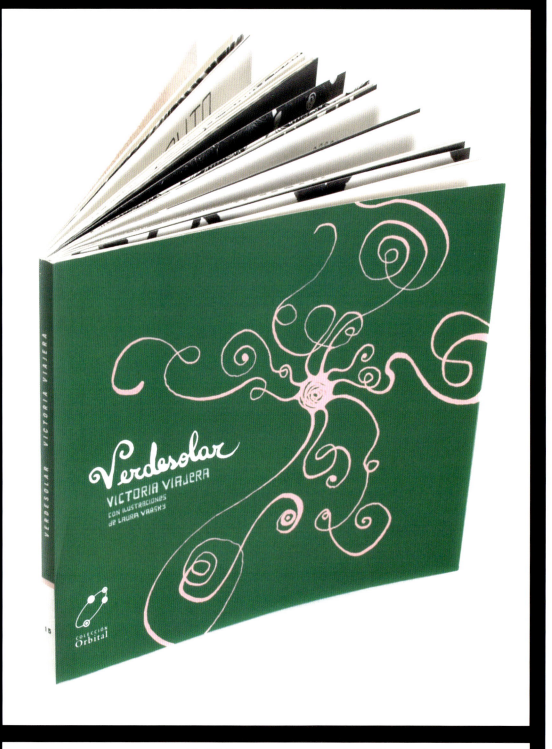

STUDIO	_CLIENT_	_DESCRIPTION_
Laura Varsky	Colección Orbital	Poetry illustrations

STUDIO	_CLIENT_	_DESCRIPTION_
Laura Varsky	Colección Orbital	Poetry illustrations

STUDIO	_CLIENT_	_DESCRIPTION_
Laura Varsky	Colección Orbital	Poetry illustrations

STUDIO	_CLIENT_	_DESCRIPTION_
Laura Varsky	Colección Orbital	Poetry illustrations

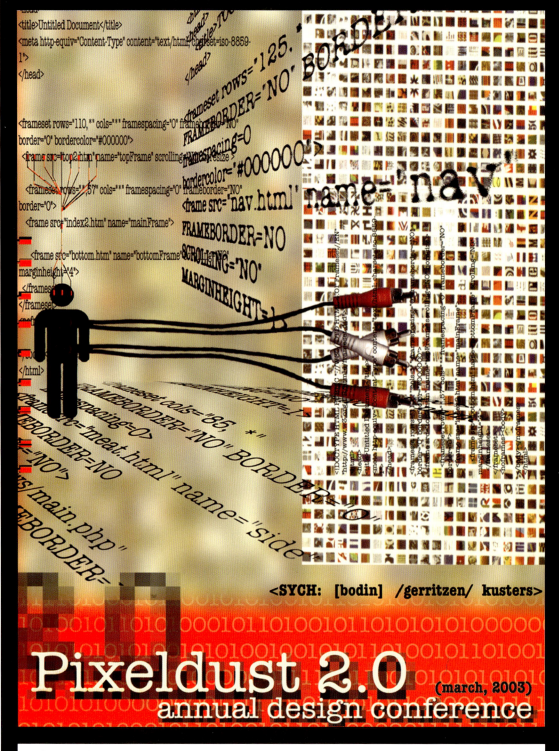

STUDIO	_CLIENT_	_DESCRIPTION_
Unmarked Vehicle	Pixeldust 2.0	Annual design conference

STUDIO	_CLIENT_	_DESCRIPTION_
Unmarked Vehicle	Pixeldust 2.0	Annual design conference

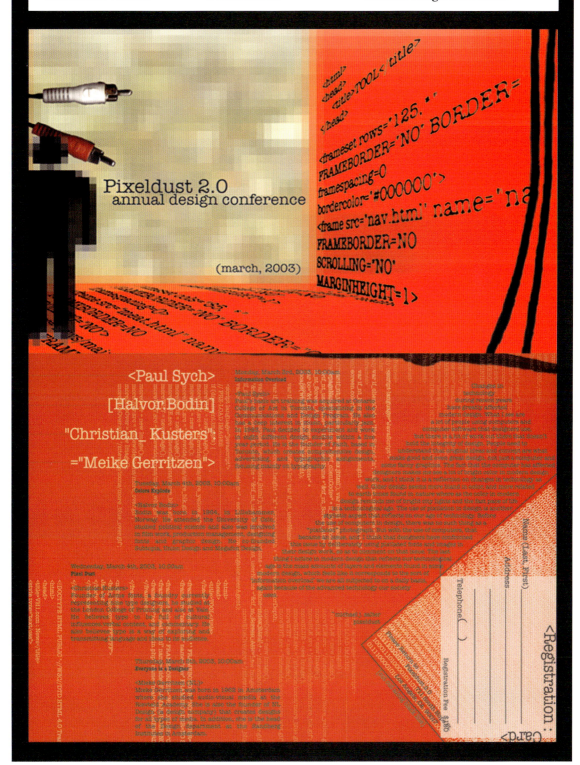

STUDIO	_CLIENT_	_DESCRIPTION_
Sagmeister Inc	The Guggenheim Museum	Art prize in New York

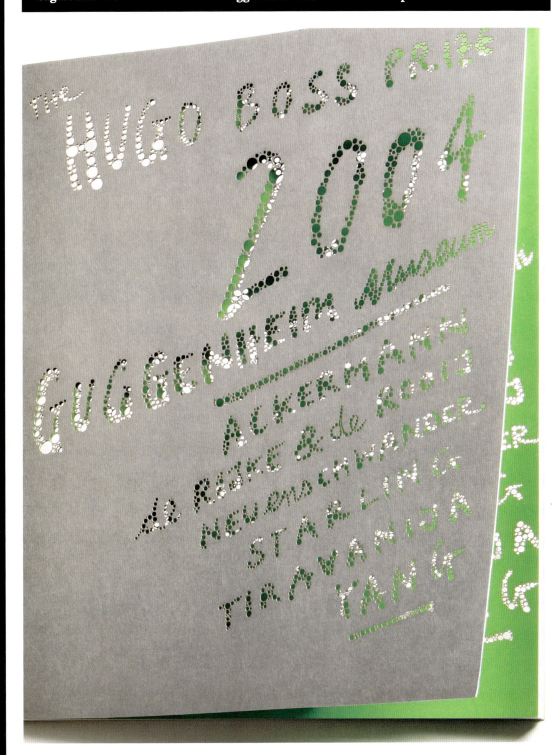

STUDIO
3rd Edge Communications

CLIENT
Revelation Generation

DESCRIPTION
Labor day weekend

STUDIO	_CLIENT_	_DESCRIPTION_
Sagmeister Inc	Sagmeister Inc	Exhibition at MAK museum

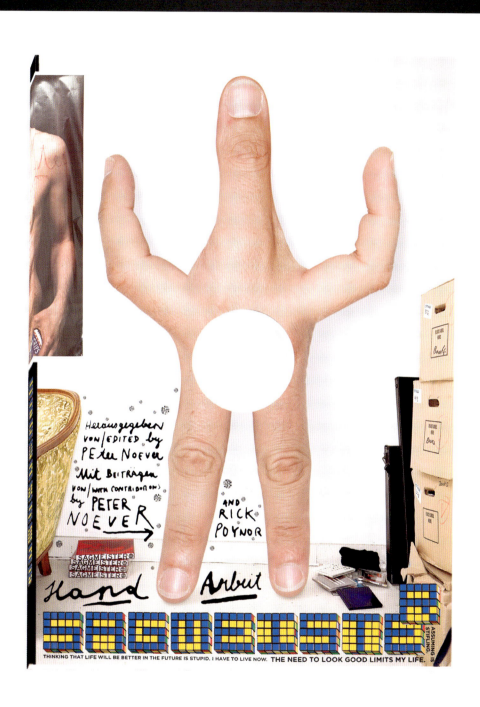

STUDIO	_CLIENT_	_DESCRIPTION_
Magma Comunicação e Design	Coppead	Graduate students portfolio

STUDIO	_CLIENT_	_DESCRIPTION_
Magma Comunicação e Design	Coppead	Graduate students portfolio

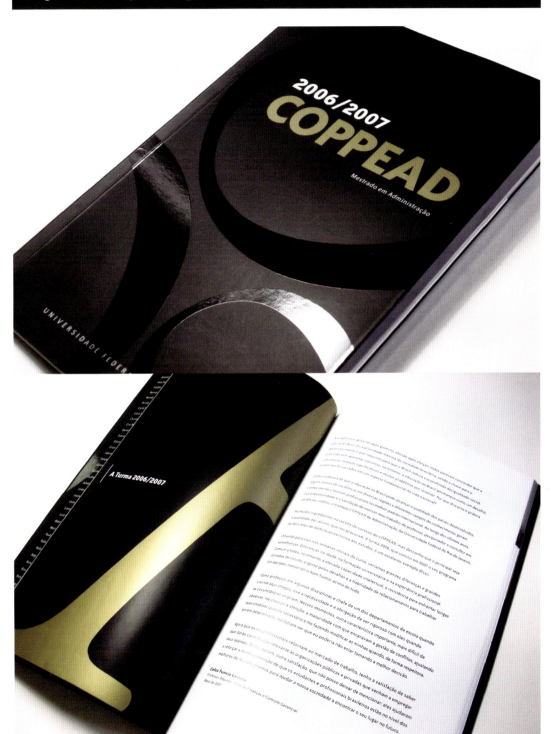

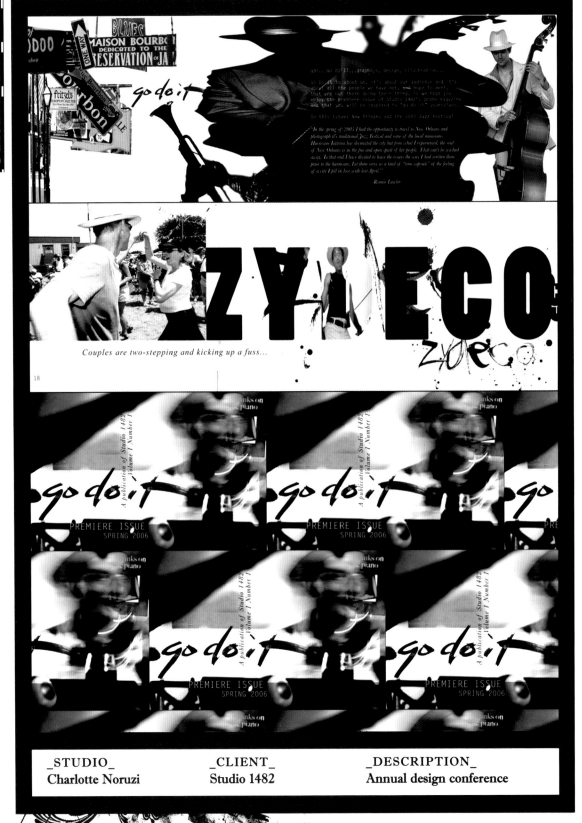

STUDIO	_CLIENT_	_DESCRIPTION_
Charlotte Noruzi	Studio 1482	Annual design conference

STUDIO	_CLIENT_	_DESCRIPTION_
Charlotte Noruzi	Studio 1482	Interview magazine issue

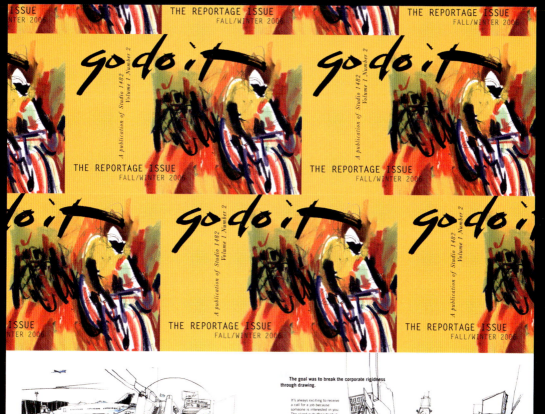

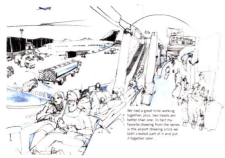

STUDIO	_CLIENT_	_DESCRIPTION_
Hyperakt Design Group	Shy Lock	Perry street theatre brochure

STUDIO
Hyperakt Design Group

CLIENT
Shy Lock

DESCRIPTION
Perry street theatre brochure

STUDIO
Archrival

CLIENT
Tip Top

DESCRIPTION
Urban living community for students

STUDIO	_CLIENT_	_DESCRIPTION_
Archrival	Tip Top	Urban living community for students

STUDIO	_CLIENT_	_DESCRIPTION_
Magma Comunicação e Design	Transpetro	Burn Prevention Campaign

STUDIO	_CLIENT_	_DESCRIPTION_
Jose Luis Guerrero Garcia	Fundación por los niños	ONG in Mexico and Colombia

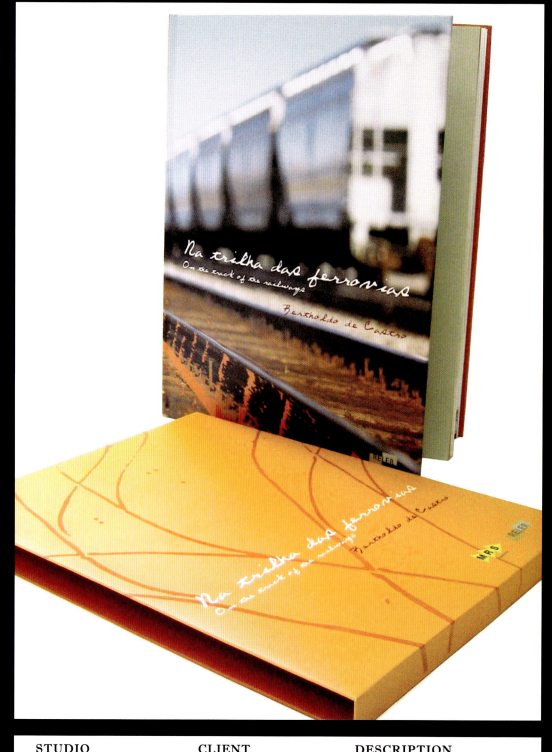

STUDIO
Redondo Design

CLIENT
Reler

DESCRIPTION
Printed material about Railways

STUDIO	_CLIENT_	_DESCRIPTION_
Redondo Design	Reler	Printed material about Railways

STUDIO	_CLIENT_	_DESCRIPTION_
Rodrigo Maciel Lima Marins	Contra Capa	Recycle materials

STUDIO	_CLIENT_	_DESCRIPTION_
Rodrigo Maciel Lima Marins	Contra Capa	Recycle materials

O plástico representa 10% do peso do lixo urbano no Brasil.
E como um bom estudante,
você precisa estar com a consciência leve.

STUDIO	_CLIENT_	_DESCRIPTION_
Rodrigo Maciel Lima Marins	Sylvio Antunes	Reality lasts

STUDIO	_CLIENT_	_DESCRIPTION_
Sebastiany Design	Fertibom	Advantages of biodiesel

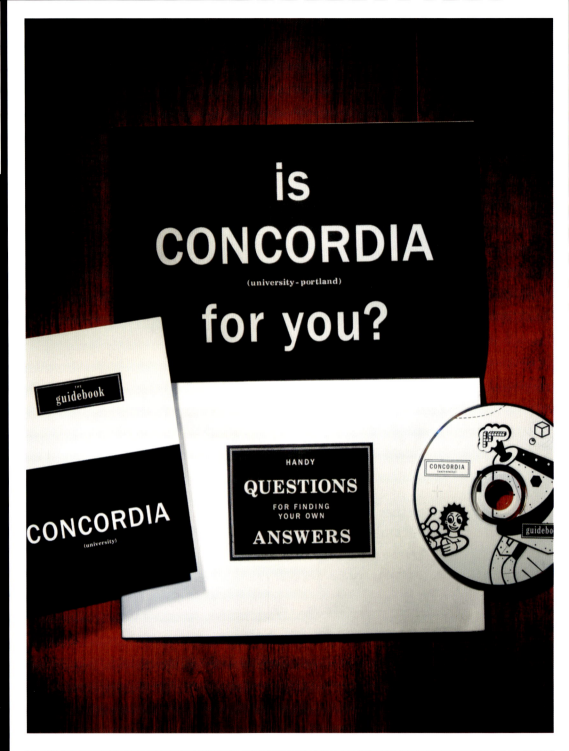

STUDIO	_CLIENT_	_DESCRIPTION_
Sockeye Creative	Concordia University	A guidebook

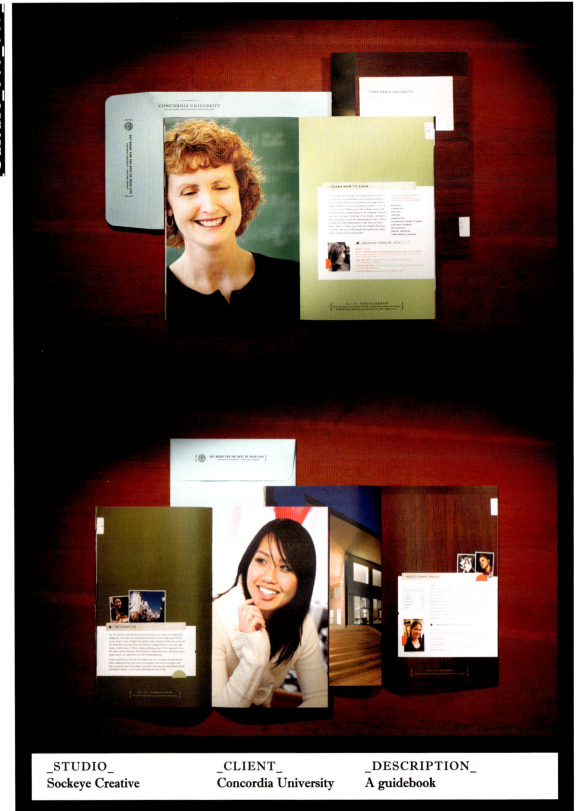

STUDIO
Sockeye Creative

CLIENT
Concordia University

DESCRIPTION
A guidebook

STUDIO	_CLIENT_	_DESCRIPTION_
Sockeye Creative	Concordia University	A guidebook

CONCORDIA UNIVERSITY

Concordia University is dedicated to the premise that spirited intellectual inquiry reinforces a commitment to compassion, justice and moral integrity. Does that sound ambitious? It is.

STUDIO	_CLIENT_	_DESCRIPTION_
Sockeye Creative	Concordia University	A guidebook

STUDIO	_CLIENT_	_DESCRIPTION_
Sockeye Creative	Concordia University	A guidebook

STUDIO	_CLIENT_	_DESCRIPTION_
Sockeye Creative	Ruby Receptionists	Recepcionist guide

STUDIO	_CLIENT_	_DESCRIPTION_
Wing Chan Design	Operation Role Models	Stay at school motivation

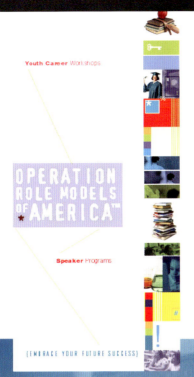

Operation Role Models of America, Inc. (ORMA) aims to motivate young people to stay in school and achieve success in their future careers. By becoming interested in a particular field, students increase their self-esteem and self-confidence, enabling them to be successful in life. ORMA exposes students to positive role models — adults with successful careers who encourage the students and provide information about their fields through speakers series presentations.

Speakers emphasize the importance of high school and college education. They tell students honestly what it takes to enter a career and to be successful in the working world. Our goal is to inspire young people to stay in school and graduate from high school. The speakers programs are our way of decreasing high school dropout rates in schools throughout the United States.

ORMA provides customized educational programs and services especially for middle and high school students. In addition, our roster of speakers is available to colleges, universities and other organizations which may be interested in finding speakers for their own events, or we can assist in creating an event for them.

STUDIO
Sockeye Creative

CLIENT
Portland S. University

DESCRIPTION
Folder of university

STUDIO	_CLIENT_	_DESCRIPTION_
Sockeye Creative	Concordia University	Folder of university

STUDIO	_CLIENT_	_DESCRIPTION_
Templin Brink Design	St. Louis Public School	Gateway courtyard

STUDIO	_CLIENT_	_DESCRIPTION_
Templin Brink Design	St. Louis Public School	Gateway courtyard

INVESTMENT SUCCESS IS HARD.

Growing an investment portfolio is hard work. Fees, taxes, transaction costs, and inflation can be relentless. Just as dangerous is the siren song of easy performance: what worked last year, the cult of manager personality, skewed headlines, investment fads, all peddling hope while ignoring harder realities. Given a choice between focusing on risk, costs, or return—most investors will exclusively choose predicting and seeking return—often to their detriment.

STUDIO	_CLIENT_	_DESCRIPTION_
Turnstyle	Parametric	Structured portfolio management

STUDIO	_CLIENT_	_DESCRIPTION_
Turnstyle	Parametric	Structured portfolio management

PARAMETRIC TAX-MANAGED CORE:
THE BEST OF BOTH WORLDS
THE CONSISTENT PERFORMANCE AND DIVERSIFICATION OF INDEX-BASED INVESTING WITH ACTIVE TAX MANAGEMENT AND CUSTOMIZATION.

- An index-based account with tax-management? **Yes.**
- A custom separate account providing "core" exposure? **Yes.**
- A natural complement to active "satellites?" **Yes.**
- A useful tool in dealing with private client issues like social restrictions, low-basis stocks, and charitable gifting strategies? **Absolutely.**

MEASURING WHAT MATTERS.

Costs and taxes can change everything—particularly for the high net worth investor. And what many advisors and their clients have come to realize is that simply measuring pre-tax performance is not good enough. Not when fees, taxes, transaction costs, and inflation can erode much, if not most, of your gains.

In the area of mutual funds, where public data is available, a recent Lipper research study showed that investors gave up—on average over the last 10 years—1.3 to 2.5 percentage points of return per year due to taxes alone.[1]

DELIVERING BETTER BETA

Investors and their advisors increasingly seek core market exposure as they structure portfolios. Consistently capturing the performance and risk attributes of a given market or market segment (or "beta") is important in delivering the benefits of asset allocation.

Index mutual funds and ETFs deliver index-tracking returns with low turnover, but as commingled investment vehicles, generally cannot be designed to accommodate an investor's taxes or provide customization. Parametric's Tax-Managed Core (TMC) portfolios represent a significant improvement—customized core exposure and a potentially lower tax bill.

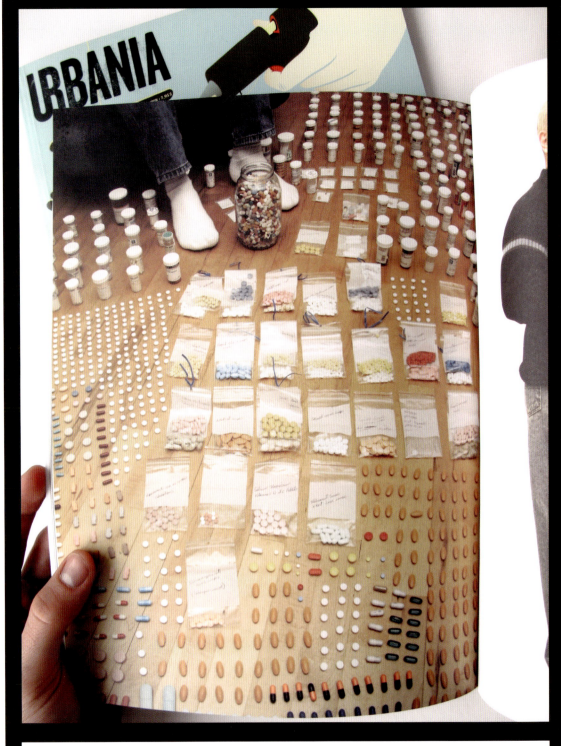

STUDIO
Karim Zariffa

CLIENT
Urbania

DESCRIPTION
Collector presentation

STUDIO	_CLIENT_	_DESCRIPTION_
Karim Zariffa	Urbania	Collector presentation

["Direct mail and trade shows are common ways to distribute brochures to introduce a product or service. In hotels and other places that tourists frequent, brochure racks or stands may suggest visits to amusement parks and other points of interest."]

STUDIO	_CLIENT_	_DESCRIPTION_
Gouthier Design	Hang Together	Employee manual

STUDIO	_CLIENT_	_DESCRIPTION_
Gouthier Design	Hang Together	Employee manual

STUDIO	_CLIENT_	_DESCRIPTION_
Gouthier Design	Graft	A journal on brand design

STUDIO	_CLIENT_	_DESCRIPTION_
Gouthier Design	Graft	A journal on brand design

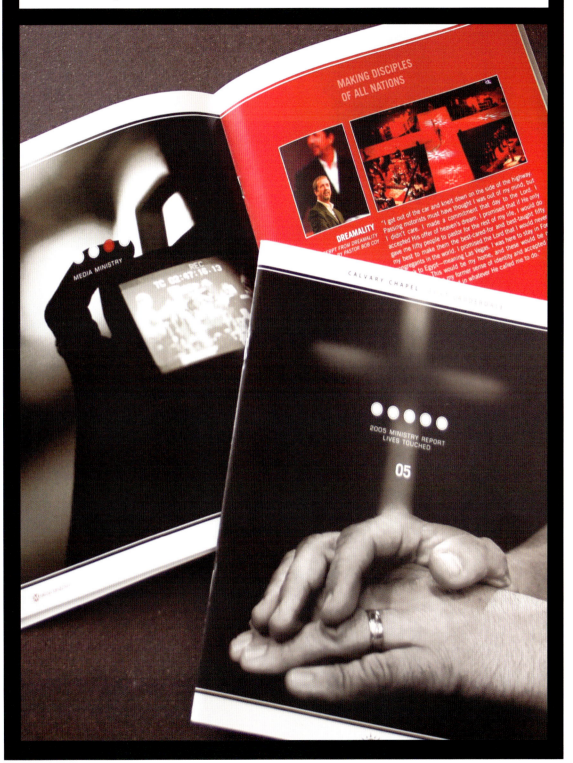

STUDIO	_CLIENT_	_DESCRIPTION_
Gouthier Design	Domani	Italian genius for living

STUDIO	_CLIENT_	_DESCRIPTION_
Gouthier Design	AR	Annual report

STUDIO	_CLIENT_	_DESCRIPTION_
Gouthier Design	Erin London	Personal brochure

STUDIO	_CLIENT_	_DESCRIPTION_
Gouthier Design	Advertising Federation	ONG folder

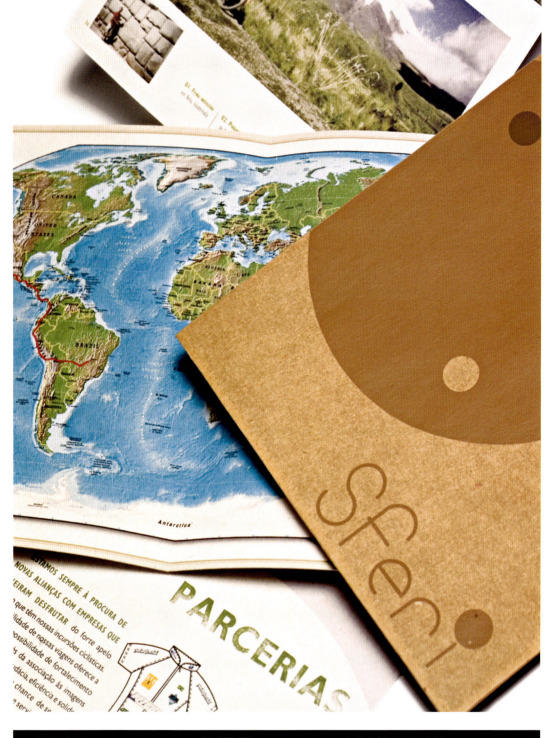

STUDIO	_CLIENT_	_DESCRIPTION_
Adriano Fidalgo	Sferi	Riding a bike from north to south

STUDIO	_CLIENT_	_DESCRIPTION_
MSLK	MSLK	Self promotion

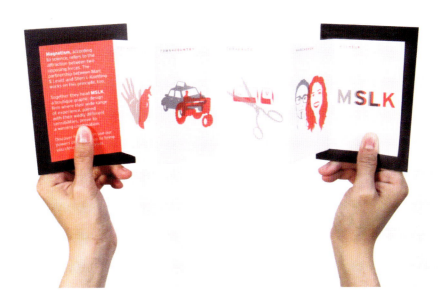

SUBSTANCE151 IS A MULTIDISCIPLINARY DESIGN FIRM THAT HELPS ORGANIZATIONS FULFILL THEIR MISSION BY BREAKING THROUGH THE MARKETPLACE CLUTTER AND DISTINGUISHING THEMSELVES — STRATEGICALLY AND VISUALLY.

STUDIO
Ida Cheinman

CLIENT
Substance 151

DESCRIPTION
Company portfolio

STUDIO	_CLIENT_	_DESCRIPTION_
Sayles Graphic Design	Sayles Graphic Design	Company business

STUDIO
Evio Design

CLIENT
Misc.

DESCRIPTION
Art brochure

STUDIO
Evio Design

CLIENT
Misc.

DESCRIPTION
Art brochure

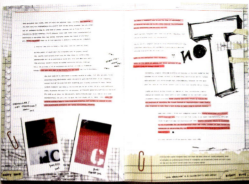

STUDIO	_CLIENT_	_DESCRIPTION_
Ida Cheinman	Advertising Assoc. of Baltimore	Game of skill

STUDIO	_CLIENT_	_DESCRIPTION_
Ida Cheinman	Advertising Assoc. of Baltimore	Game of skill

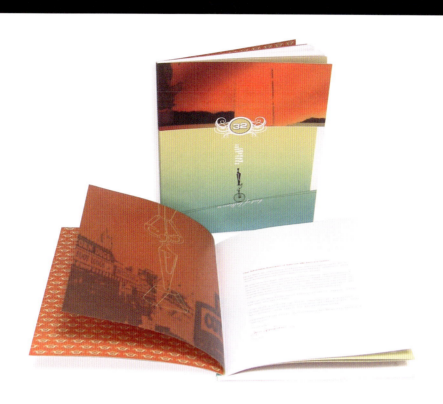

SOON, IF NOT ALREADY, EVERYTHING WILL BE DESIGNED. PEOPLE, PLACES, THINGS, EXPERIENCES. IT'S ONLY A MATTER OF WHEN, HOW WELL, AND TO WHAT END. WHO DESIGNS ALL THIS STUFF? EVERYONE'S A DESIGNER. NOT ENOUGH DESIGNERS. WHAT WE MAKE, WE DESIGN. WHAT WE EDIT, PLAN, FIX, OR REMODEL, WE DESIGN. WHAT WE TOUCH, WE DESIGN. QUALITY OF DESIGN DETERMINES THE QUALITY OF OUR LIVES. LOOK AROUND. CONSIDER HOW YOU DEFINE DESIGN. MAKE THINGS BETTER. MAKE BETTER THINGS.

AIGA DETROIT DESIGN REVIEW 05

AIGA Detroit Chapter

STUDIO
BBK Studio

CLIENT
AIGA

DESCRIPTION
Detroit design review 05

STUDIO	_CLIENT_	_DESCRIPTION_
BBK Studio	AIGA	Detroit design review 05

STUDIO
BBK Studio

CLIENT
AIGA

DESCRIPTION
Detroit design review 05

STUDIO	_CLIENT_	_DESCRIPTION_
BBK Studio	AIGA	Detroit design review 05

STUDIO	_CLIENT_	_DESCRIPTION_
BBK Studio	AIGA	Detroit design review 05

STUDIO	_CLIENT_	_DESCRIPTION_
BBK Studio	AIGA	Detroit design review 05

STUDIO
Nicola Place

CLIENT
Design by Build

DESCRIPTION
Folder opened

STUDIO	_CLIENT_	_DESCRIPTION_
Nicola Place	Design by Build	Book presentation

STUDIO
Blok Design

CLIENT
A! Diseño

DESCRIPTION
Internacional awards

STUDIO	_CLIENT_	_DESCRIPTION_
Blok Design	A! Diseño	Internacional awards

PU
DE
DE

MATTHEW C
RAFAEL ESQ
VINCE FROS
REINHARD G
EIKO ISHIOK

ANNETTE KF
PIERRE MEN

INTERCAMBIO / INTERCONEXIÓN / INTERCULTURAL / INTE

INT

12 CONFERENCIA INTERNACIONAL Y PREMIO a! DISEÑO

Octubre 30 a noviembre 2

Renovarse o morir, dirían algunos. Para nosotros es generar la doceava Conferencia Internacional basada en **"PUNTOS DE INTERACCIÓN"**, que nos motiven a ver más allá del horizonte actual, creer profundamente que el diseño puede cambiar nuestro entorno, reconocer que el diseño es la palanca que mueve la rueda de la economía mundial, ayudar a que las vidas mejoren gracias al diseño… Recordar que por eso elegimos esta profesión. Si existen fanáticos en cualquier área, ¿por qué no ser fanáticos del diseño? Invitamos a aquellos que deseen interactuar junto a diseñadores comprometidos de Alemania, Australia, Austria, Estados Unidos, Irán, Japón y por supuesto de México, en un evento verdaderamente único que no podrás perderte.

El diseño es pasión…

En **"PUNTOS DE INTERACCIÓN"** experimentaremos emoción, sensibilidad, inspiración, actualización, nuevos colores, percepciones diversas, nuevos ambientes; veremos al mundo de manera distinta, cargaremos pilas y volveremos a decir: jamás lo había imaginado…

INFO. T (55) 5679-3040 | F (55) 5679-3166 | www.a.com.mx | pd@a.com.mx

PREMIO INTERNACIONAL a! DISEÑO 2004

Convocatoria

Podrán participar profesionales y estudiantes de las carreras de diseño gráfico, diseño industrial, arquitectura, diseño textil, publicidad, mercadotecnia, comunicación y fotografía de México y del extranjero.

Recepción de trabajos y fecha límite

La recepción de trabajos será en: Hacienda de la Escalera No. 22, Col. Prado Coapa, México D.F., 14350. T: (55) 5679 3040 F: (55) 5679 3166. Fecha límite para recepción de trabajos: **15 DE OCTUBRE**.

Cuota de inscripción

Profesionales	$375.00
Suscriptores activos de a! Diseño	$350.00
Estudiantes	$200.00

Consulta las categorías para profesionales y estudiantes, y la forma de inscripción en www.a.com.mx

Entrega de premios

1 de agosto, 12:30 hrs. Hotel Fiesta Americana, Querétaro. Entrada libre.

OCT 15

STUDIO	_CLIENT_	_DESCRIPTION_
Blok Design	El Zanjon	Architecture presentation

STUDIO	_CLIENT_	_DESCRIPTION_
MSLK	Judith Miller	Images to inspire

STUDIO	_CLIENT_	_DESCRIPTION_
Turnstyle	Teague 80	8 decades of influential design

STUDIO	_CLIENT_	_DESCRIPTION_
Turnstyle	Teague 80	8 decades of influential design

STUDIO
Turnstyle

CLIENT
Teague 80

DESCRIPTION
Design this days folder

STUDIO	_CLIENT_	_DESCRIPTION_
Turnstyle	Teague 80	Design this days folder

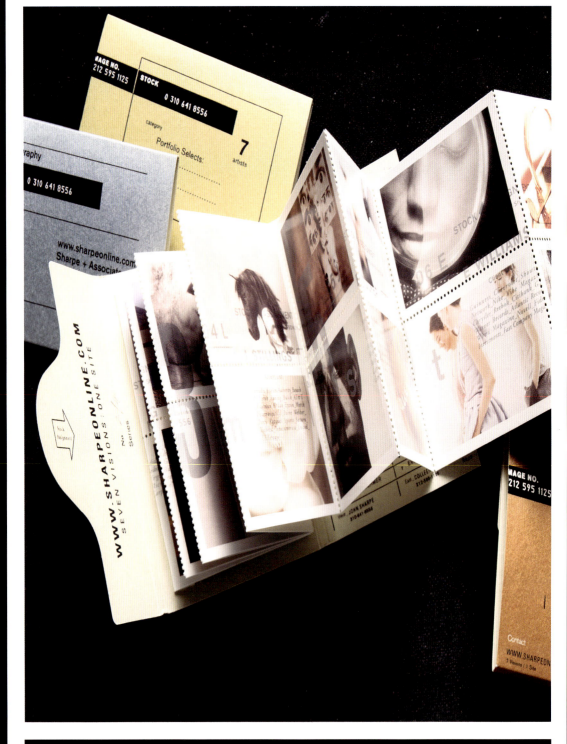

STUDIO
Templin Brink Design

CLIENT
Sharpeonline

DESCRIPTION
Company Folder

STUDIO	_CLIENT_	_DESCRIPTION_
Templin Brink Design	Art Real	Screen printing

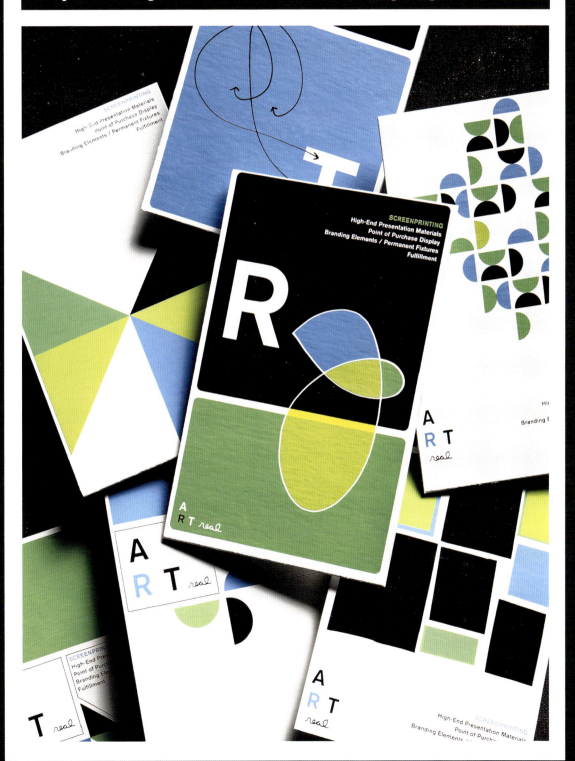

Protosynthesis

A talk about how T.B. D. germinates a concept, then watches it grow.

Join Templin Brink Design principals Joel Templin and Gaby Brink, as they share how their studio has developed a highly effective ideation process. They will walk through a variety of projects, from start to finish, revealing the nourishment it takes to cultivate a concept into an effective finished product.

Since opening their doors in 1998, Templin Brink Design has created highly original and effective branding, packaging, corporate identity and advertising campaigns for top global marketers like American Eagle Outfitters, Apple Computer, Cisco, Coca-Cola, Dockers / Levi's, Janus Capital Group, Lucent Technologies, Oracle, Target Stores, and Williams-Sonoma.

STUDIO	_CLIENT_	_DESCRIPTION_
Templin Brink Design	AIGA	Protosynthesis, ideation process

STUDIO	_CLIENT_	_DESCRIPTION_
Templin Brink Design	Friend & Johnson	Portfolio brochure

print

STUDIO	_CLIENT_	_DESCRIPTION_
Julien Vallée	Print	Brochure of cult design

STUDIO	_CLIENT_	_DESCRIPTION_
Julien Vallée	Print	Brochure of cult design

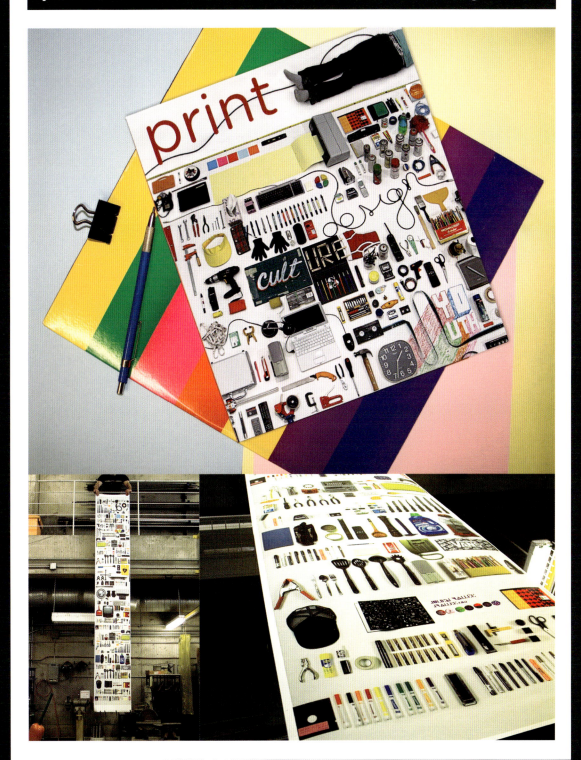

STUDIO	_CLIENT_	_DESCRIPTION_
Sagmeister Inc	Zumtobel AG	Lighting systems

STUDIO	_CLIENT_	_DESCRIPTION_
Sagmeister Inc	Zumtobel AG	Lighting systems

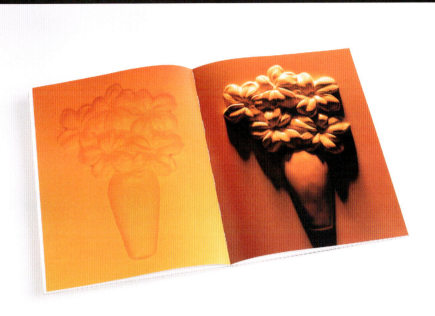

STUDIO	_CLIENT_	_DESCRIPTION_
Sagmeister Inc	American Institure G.A.	Conference of graphic arts

STUDIO	_CLIENT_	_DESCRIPTION_
Sagmeister Inc	Booth Clibborn Editions	Brochure Made you look

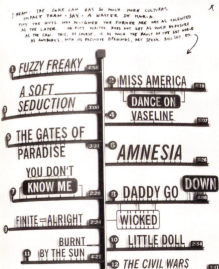

STUDIO
Sagmeister Inc

CLIENT
Sagmeister Inc

DESCRIPTION
Exhibitions in different places

STUDIO	_CLIENT_	_DESCRIPTION_
Sagmeister Inc	Sagmeister Inc	Grafical experimentations

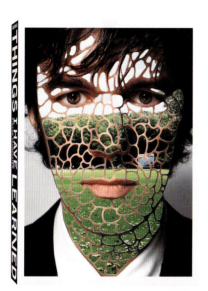
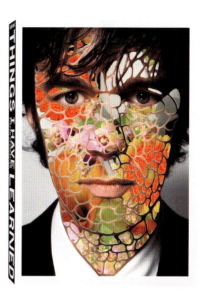
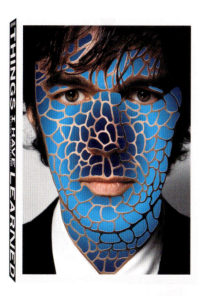
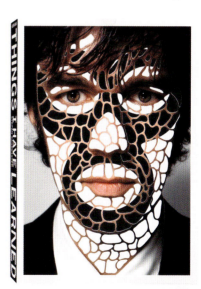

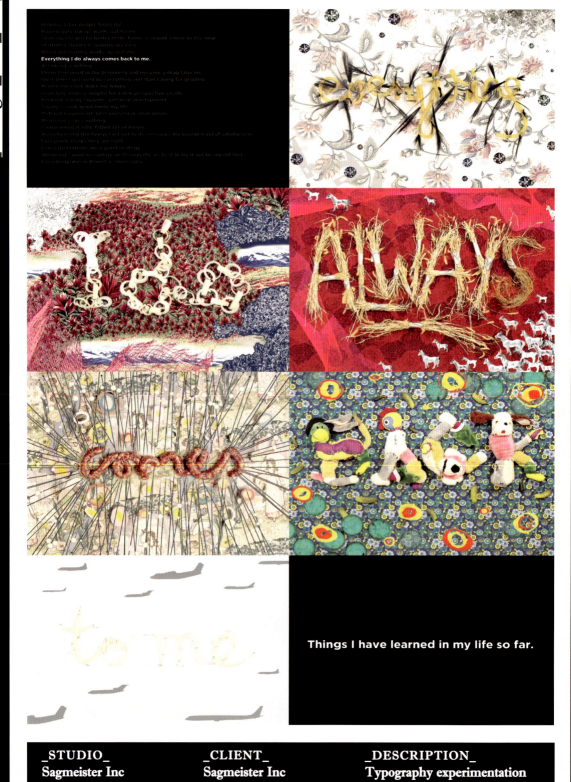

Things I have learned in my life so far.

STUDIO
Sagmeister Inc

CLIENT
Sagmeister Inc

DESCRIPTION
Typography experimentation

STUDIO	_CLIENT_	_DESCRIPTION_
Sagmeister Inc	Sagmeister Inc	Typography experimentation

Helping other people helps me.
Having guts always works out for me.
Thinking life will be better in the future is stupid, I have to live now.
Starting a charity is surprisingly easy.
Being not truthful works against me.
Everything I do always comes back to me.
Assuming is stifling.
Drugs feel great in the beginning and become a drag later on.
Over time I get used to everything and start taking for granted.
Money does not make me happy.
Traveling alone is helpful for a new perspective on life.
Keeping a diary supports personal development.
Trying to look good limits my life.
Material luxuries are best enjoyed in small doses.
Worrying solves nothing.
Complaining is silly. Either act or forget.
Actually doing the things I set out to do increases my overall level of satisfaction.
Everybody thinks they are right.
Low expectations are a good strategy.
Whatever I want to explore professionally, its best to try it out for myself first.
Everybody who is honest is interesting.

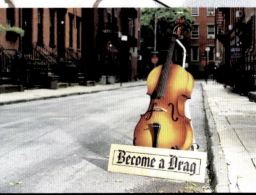

STUDIO
Karim Zariffa

CLIENT
UQAM

DESCRIPTION
Graphical experimentation

STUDIO	_CLIENT_	_DESCRIPTION_
Karim Zariffa	UQAM	Graphical experimentation

STUDIO	_CLIENT_	_DESCRIPTION_
Karim Zariffa	UQAM	Graphical Experimentation

STUDIO
Karim Zariffa

CLIENT
UQAM

DESCRIPTION
Graphical experimentation

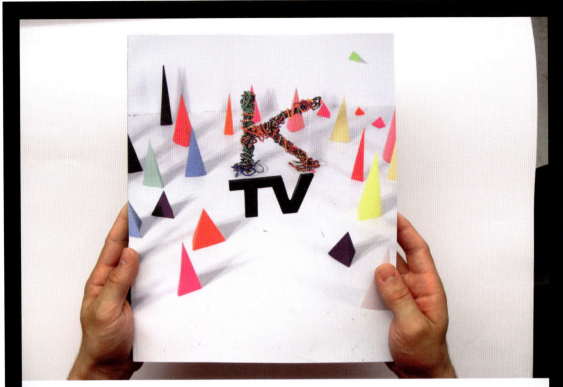

STUDIO	_CLIENT_	_DESCRIPTION_
Karim Zariffa	UQAM	Making of KTV

STUDIO	_CLIENT_	_DESCRIPTION_
Karim Zariffa	UQAM	Making of KTV

STUDIO	_CLIENT_	_DESCRIPTION_
Delrancho	Universidad del Pacífico	Art direction + good intentions

STUDIO
Delrancho

CLIENT
Universidad del Pacífico

DESCRIPTION
Art direction + good intentions

STUDIO
Sifon

CLIENT
TDI

DESCRIPTION
Tecnology, design and innovation

| _STUDIO_ | _CLIENT_ | _DESCRIPTION_ |
| Sifon | TDI | Tecnology, design and innovation |

STUDIO
Sifon

CLIENT
TDI

DESCRIPTION
Tecnology, design and innovation

STUDIO	_CLIENT_	_DESCRIPTION_
Sifon	TDI	Tecnology, design and innovation

STUDIO	_CLIENT_	_DESCRIPTION_
Sifon	TDI	Tecnology, design and innovation

STUDIO	_CLIENT_	_DESCRIPTION_
Sifon	TDI	Tecnology, design and innovation

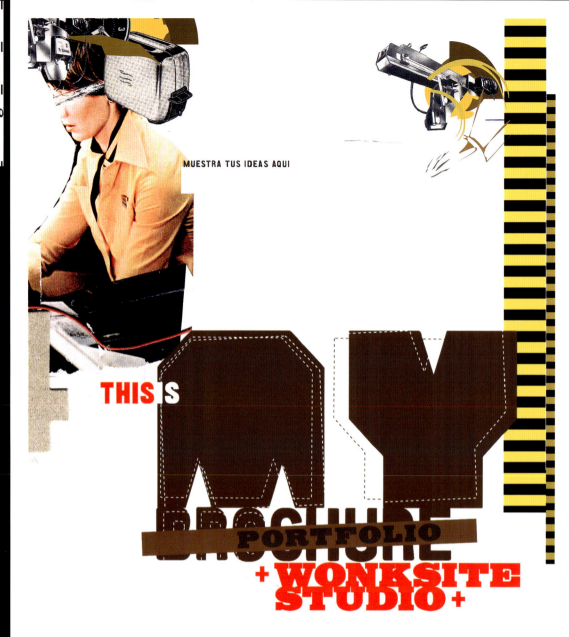

STUDIO	_CLIENT_	_DESCRIPTION_
Wonksite Studio	Jorge Restrepo	Portfolio / Corporate brochure

STUDIO	_CLIENT_	_DESCRIPTION_
Wonksite Studio	Jorge Restrepo	Portfolio / Corporate brochure

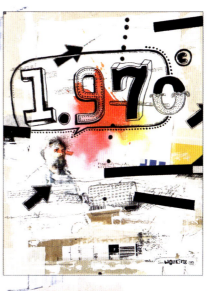

08.THE THIRD WAY/ COMPUTER ARTS / MAGAZINE ILLUSTRATION / U.K. + **09.FONT MANAGEMENT** / COMPUTER ARTS PROJECTS/ MAGAZINE ILLUSTRATION / U.K. + **10.MARÍA LLENA ERES DE GRACIA** / BLANK MAGAZINE / ILLUSTRATION / CHILE. **11.HELVETICA. BIOGRAPHY OF A FONT** / LINOTYPE / POSTER / U.S.A. + **12.MY FAVORITE TOY** / MASTERS OF PHOTOSHOP VOL. 2 / COAUTHOR / U.S.A. + **13.PECHAKUCHANIGHT VOL. 3** / PECHAKUCHANIGHT / POSTER ILLUSTRATION / COLOMBIA.

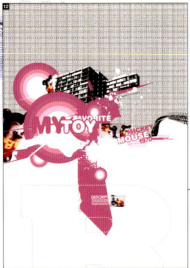

STUDIO
Wonksite Studio

CLIENT
Jorge Restrepo

DESCRIPTION
Portfolio / Corporate brochure

STUDIO	_CLIENT_	_DESCRIPTION_
Wonksite Studio	Jorge Restrepo	Portfolio / Corporate brochure

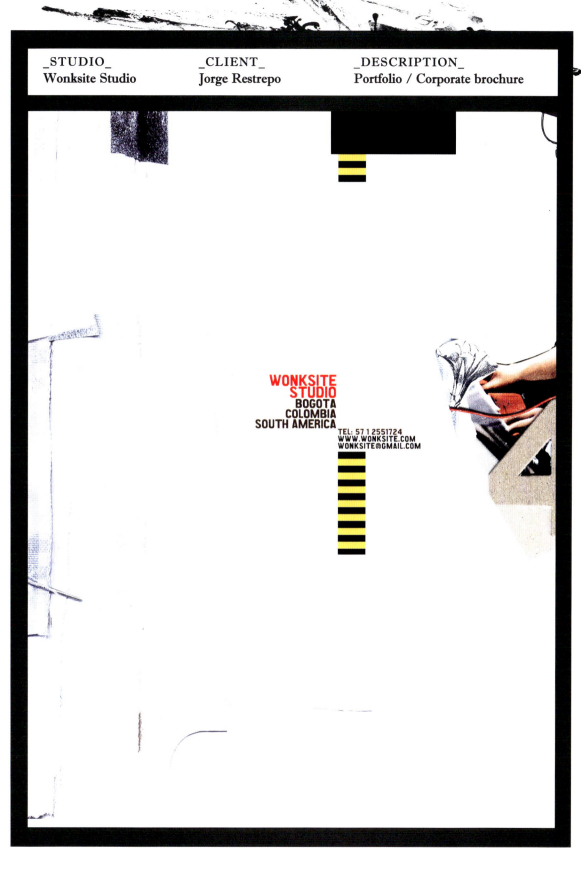

STUDIO
Savio Alphonso

CLIENT
Grand Central Press

DESCRIPTION
Artist Catalog for Laurie Hassold

STUDIO	_CLIENT_	_DESCRIPTION_
Savio Alphonso	Grand Central Press	Artist Catalog for Laurie Hassold

STUDIO	_CLIENT_	_DESCRIPTION_
Sayles Graphic Design	Sayles Graphic Design	Advertisement federation of Fargo

STUDIO	_CLIENT_	_DESCRIPTION_
Sayles Graphic Design	Sayles Graphic Design	Kansas City Ad Club

["Two of the most common brochure styles are single-sheet and booklet forms. A common single-sheet brochure is double-sided (printed on both sides) and folded into thirds."]

ENTERTAINMENT

STUDIO	_CLIENT_	_DESCRIPTION_
Archrival	Red Bull	World car series championship

STUDIO	_CLIENT_	_DESCRIPTION_
Archrival	Red Bull	World car series championship

STUDIO
Archrival

CLIENT
Red Bull

DESCRIPTION
World car series championship

STUDIO	_CLIENT_	_DESCRIPTION_
Archrival	Red Bull	World car series championship

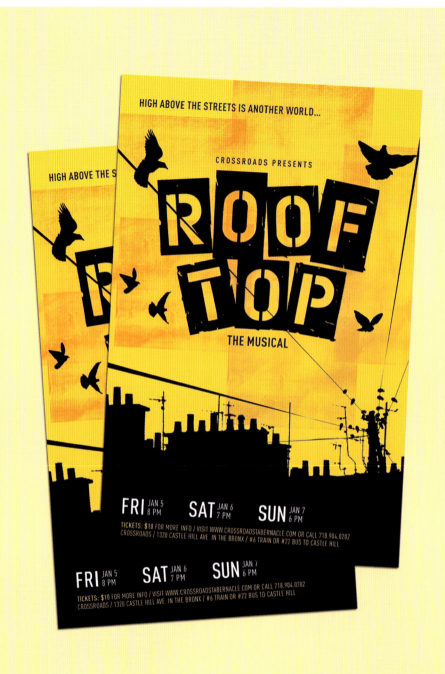

STUDIO
3rd Edge Communications

CLIENT
Roof Top

DESCRIPTION
Musical brochure

STUDIO	_CLIENT_	_DESCRIPTION_
3rd Edge Communications	Crossroads	Hiphop performance brochure

STUDIO	_CLIENT_	_DESCRIPTION_
3rd Edge Communications	Eagles Valley	Resort folder

STUDIO
3rd Edge Communications

CLIENT
RA Travel

DESCRIPTION
Travel services folder

STUDIO
Gouthier Design

CLIENT
Anchor Club

DESCRIPTION
Club brochure

STUDIO	_CLIENT_	_DESCRIPTION_
Laura Varsky	Arbol	Music event

STUDIO	_CLIENT_	_DESCRIPTION_
Sangre.tv	CIE	Radio broadcasting group

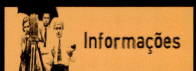

STUDIO
Matrix - Breno Carvalho

CLIENT
Socine

DESCRIPTION
Film and movie festival

STUDIO	_CLIENT_	_DESCRIPTION_
Sangre.tv	Animascope	50s brochure

STUDIO	_CLIENT_	_DESCRIPTION_
Rodrigo Maciel Lima Marins	Psigama 06	Psychology workshop

STUDIO	_CLIENT_	_DESCRIPTION_
Sangre.tv	Radioset	A bar with live radio broadcast

STUDIO
Mujica TMP

CLIENT
Frente de Danza Independiente

DESCRIPTION
Young choreography festival

STUDIO	_CLIENT_	_DESCRIPTION_
Hyperakt Design Group	Brooklyn Bridge Park	Movies in motion

STUDIO
Hyperakt Design Group

CLIENT
Brooklyn Arts Council

DESCRIPTION
Cultural after school adventure

STUDIO
Hyperakt Design Group

CLIENT
Brooklyn Arts Council

DESCRIPTION
Cultural after school adventure

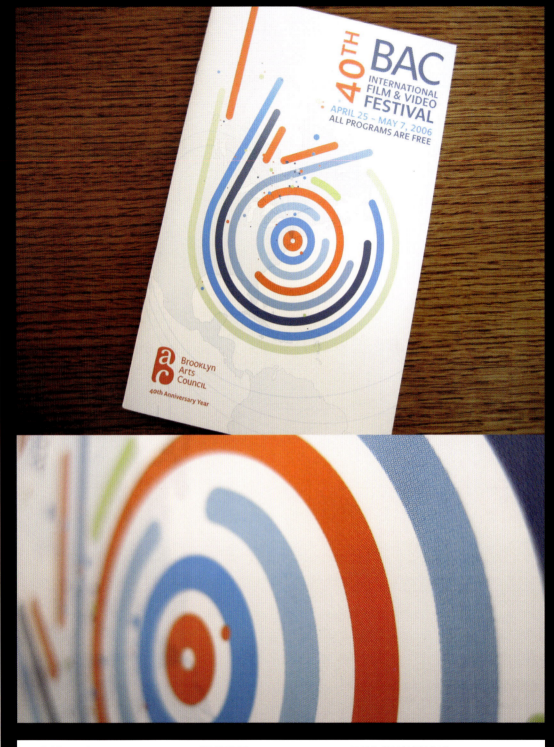

STUDIO	_CLIENT_	_DESCRIPTION_
Hyperakt Design Group	Brooklyn Arts Council	Internacional film & movie festival

STUDIO	_CLIENT_	_DESCRIPTION_
Hyperakt Design Group	Brooklyn Arts Council	Internacional film & movie festival

STUDIO
Hyperakt Design Group

CLIENT
Brooklyn Bridge Park

DESCRIPTION
Real estate lauch

STUDIO	_CLIENT_	_DESCRIPTION_
Hyperakt Design Group	Brooklyn Bridge Park	Real estate lauch

STUDIO	_CLIENT_	_DESCRIPTION_
Hyperakt Design Group	Brooklyn Bridge Park	Sunset Bouzouki

STUDIO	_CLIENT_	_DESCRIPTION_
Hyperakt Design Group	Brooklyn Bridge Park	Sunset Bouzouki

STUDIO	_CLIENT_	_DESCRIPTION_
Hyperakt Design Group	Firehouse 735	Real Estate prospect heights

STUDIO
Hyperakt Design Group

CLIENT
Firehouse 735

DESCRIPTION
Real Estate prospect heights

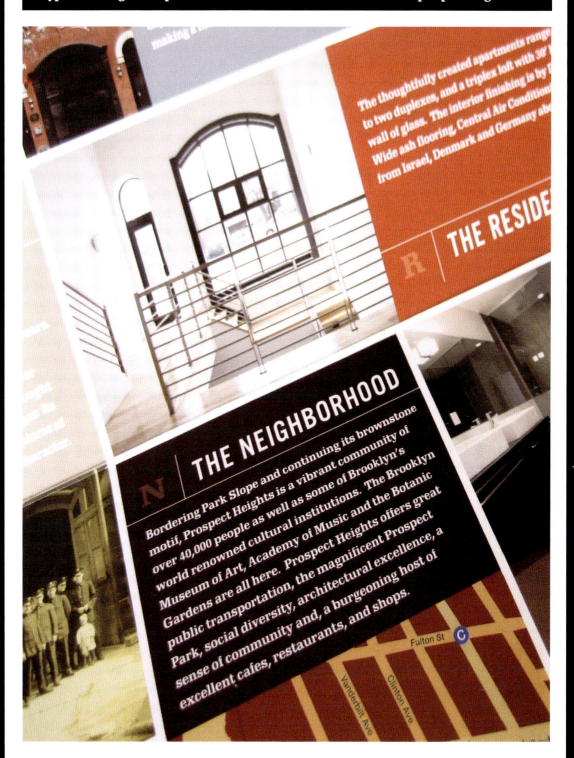

STUDIO	_CLIENT_	_DESCRIPTION_
Hyperakt Design Group	More NYC	Tourist information brochure

STUDIO	_CLIENT_	_DESCRIPTION_
Hyperakt Design Group	More NYC	Tourist information brochure

STUDIO	_CLIENT_	_DESCRIPTION_
Hyperakt Design Group	More NYC	Tourist information brochure

| _STUDIO_ | _CLIENT_ | _DESCRIPTION_ |
| Hyperakt Design Group | More NYC | Tourist information brochure |

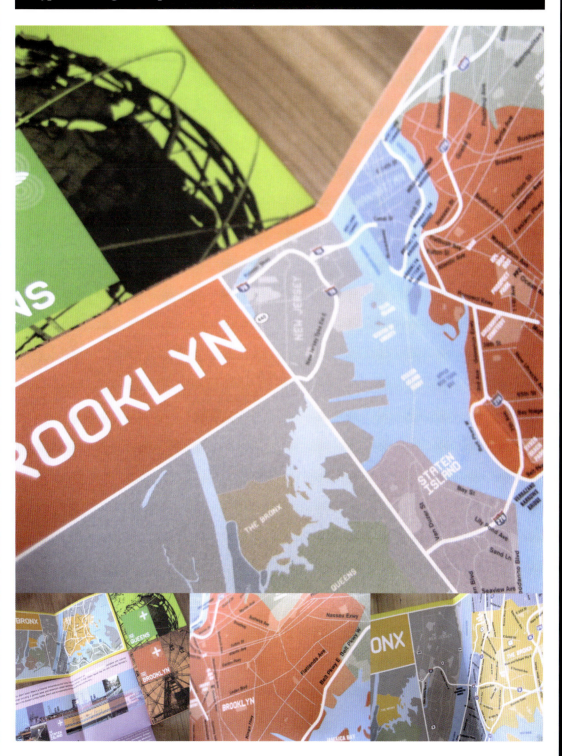

STUDIO	_CLIENT_	_DESCRIPTION_
Valeria Prada	Viart	Latinamerican festival

STUDIO	_CLIENT_	_DESCRIPTION_
Sockeye Creative	Game Crazy	The brand legacy

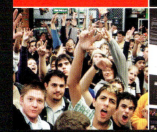

STUDIO
Guerrilha CT

CLIENT
Fundação Roberto Marinho

DESCRIPTION
Turism development

STUDIO	_CLIENT_	_DESCRIPTION_
Guerrilha CT	Fundação Roberto Marinho	Turism development

STUDIO	_CLIENT_	_DESCRIPTION_
Laranja Design	IPB News	Fashion meeting brochure

STUDIO	_CLIENT_	_DESCRIPTION_
Sagmeister Inc	Anni Kuan	Fashion brochure

HAPPILY INVITES YOU TO PREVIEW THE FALL AND WINTER 2008 COLLECTION AT THE FASHION COTERIE FROM SUNDAY, FEBRUARY 10th TO TUESDAY, FEBRUARY 12th 2008, THE JAVITS CENTER, NEW YORK CITY.

STUDIO	_CLIENT_	_DESCRIPTION_
Sagmeister Inc	Anni Kuan	Fashion brochure

STUDIO	_CLIENT_	_DESCRIPTION_
Sagmeister Inc	Anni Kuan	Fashion brochure

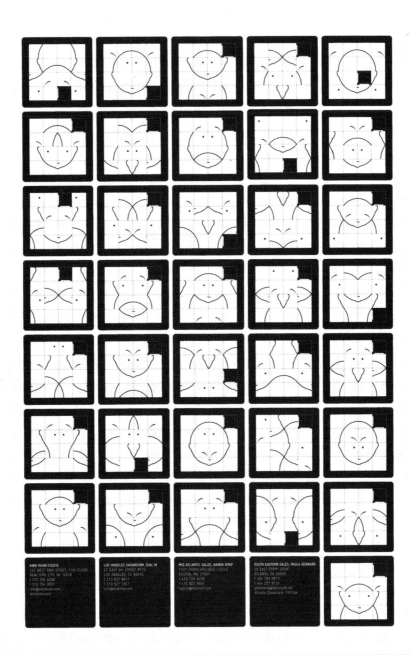

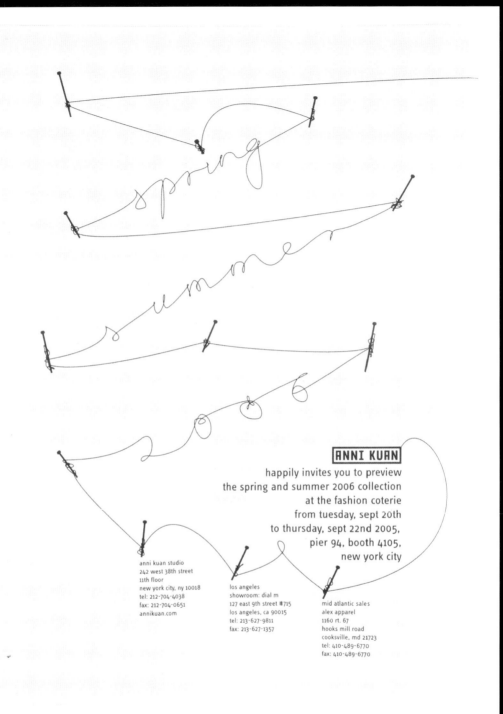

STUDIO
Sagmeister Inc

CLIENT
Anni Kuan

DESCRIPTION
Fashion brochure

STUDIO	_CLIENT_	_DESCRIPTION_
Sagmeister Inc	Anni Kuan	Fashion brochure

STUDIO	_CLIENT_	_DESCRIPTION_
Sagmeister Inc	Anni Kuan	Fashion brochure

STUDIO	_CLIENT_	_DESCRIPTION_
Sagmeister Inc	Anni Kuan	Fashion brochure

STUDIO
Sangre.tv

CLIENT
Flehner Films Cine

DESCRIPTION
Cannes film festival brochure

STUDIO
Sangre.tv

CLIENT
Flehner Films Cine

DESCRIPTION
Film production company

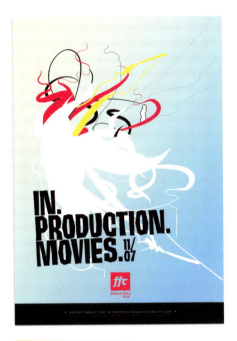

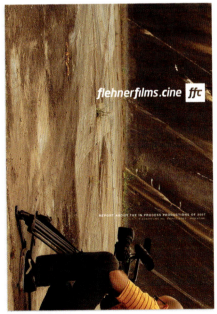

STUDIO	_CLIENT_	_DESCRIPTION_
Hybrid Design	Nike	World Cup Team

STUDIO	_CLIENT_	_DESCRIPTION_
Hybrid Design	Nike	World Cup Team

STUDIO
Mid west is best

CLIENT
NY Times

DESCRIPTION
Printed material fashion brand

STUDIO	_CLIENT_	_DESCRIPTION_
Mid west is best	NY Times	Printed material fashion brand

["The layout of the brochure will dictate whether an accordion or "Z-fold" method, the "C-fold" method, or another folding arrangement is appropriate."]

STUDIO	_CLIENT_	_DESCRIPTION_
Unmarked Vehicle	MJ	Desert brochure

STUDIO	_CLIENT_	_DESCRIPTION_
Unmarked Vehicle	MJ	Meal brochure

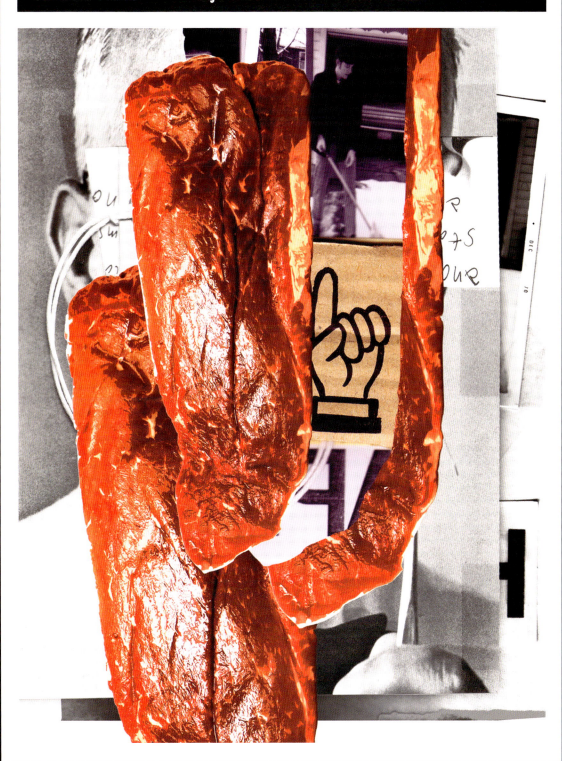

STUDIO	_CLIENT_	_DESCRIPTION_
Hyperakt Design Group	Eyecandy Images	Promotional material

STUDIO
Redcafé Comunicação

CLIENT
Granfino

DESCRIPTION
Prescriptions of success

STUDIO
Veronica Ettedgui

CLIENT
Danubio

DESCRIPTION
Pasteleria brochure

STUDIO	_CLIENT_	_DESCRIPTION_
Mario Fuentes	**Heineken**	**Beer promotional material**

STUDIO	_CLIENT_	_DESCRIPTION_
Mario Fuentes	Heineken	Beer promotional material

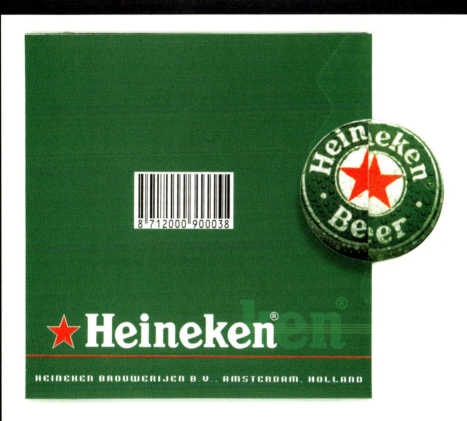

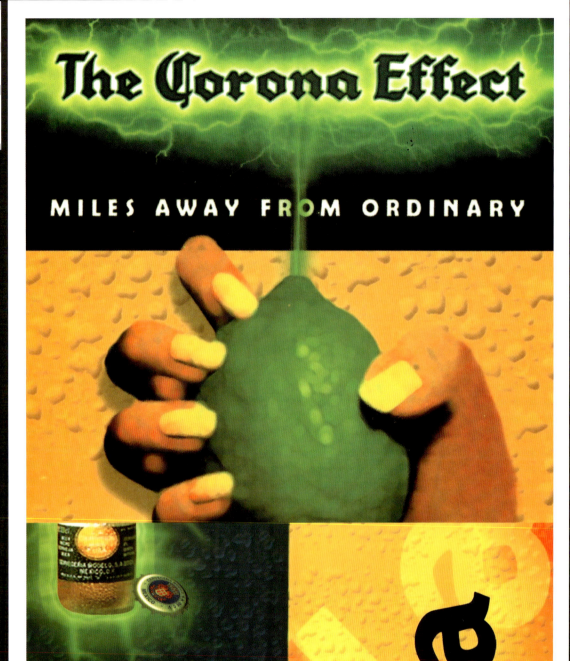

STUDIO	_CLIENT_	_DESCRIPTION_
Mario Fuentes	Corona	Mexican beer

STUDIO
Harcus Design

CLIENT
Yalumba

DESCRIPTION
Wine presentation

STUDIO	_CLIENT_	_DESCRIPTION_
Harcus Design	Yalumba	Wine presentation

PIPERS BROOK VINEYARD
TASMANIA

41°

The combination of latitude and maritime climate gives Tasmania a unique environment in which to ripen the noble grape varieties and produce prestige sparkling wines.

MODERN PIONEERS

Our world class wines have their origins in the pristine environment of the island state of Tasmania – the air, and cool, deep waters surrounding this southern landfall are amongst the purest in the world.

42°

Two hundred hectares of vineyards are located below 200 metres of altitude on the north coast of Tasmania at Pipers Brook and on the banks of the Tamar River just north of Launceston. The climate of the coastal vineyards is cooler than the Tamar vineyards, allowing us the luxury of choice for perfect sites to match grape varieties and styles. Fragrant aromatics and minerally chardonnay and pinot noir thrive in the cooler regions of Pipers Brook, whilst the warmer slopes of the Tamar River perfectly express the opulence of merlot and cabernet sauvignon.

43°
LATITUDE (S)

From vine to bottle, our skilled and dedicated winemaking team aim to fully express the distinctive characteristics of each of our vineyards.

UNIQUE COOL CLIMATE

The home of the estate is at the original Pipers Brook vineyard. Here the influence and legacy of nearby landmark, extinct volcano Mount Arthur, is clear. Red ferrosol soils provide deep, fertile and well-drained growing conditions for our cool climate specialties.

Our eight vineyards in northern Tasmania are intensively trained with close-planted Scott Henry systems or Lyre trellises. These maximise light interception and fruit exposure, leading to consistent and even fruit ripening. Characteristically, the long, slow ripening period of the region produces wines of excellent structure and flavour intensity.

STUDIO	_CLIENT_	_DESCRIPTION_
Harcus Design	Pipers Brook - Tasmania	Vineyard presentation

STUDIO	_CLIENT_	_DESCRIPTION_
Harcus Design	Ninth Island - Tasmania	Vineyard presentation

TASMANIA

NINTH 9 ISLAND

LIMESTONE COAST

Ninth Island | Australia's Coolest Wines

The pristine environments of both Tasmania and the Limestone Coast have produced a range of wines celebrating their unique and distinctive characteristics. Whether the wine is a clean crisp white, premium sparkling or a soft full-bodied red, each is a true reflection of its birthplace.

Tasmania is justly famous for its outstanding cool climate wines, particularly pinot noir, chardonnay and sparkling wines. The island's sunny but mild ripening conditions bestow a particular finesse and clarity of flavour to the grapes and express the unique character of the Tasmanian microclimate. The wines reap the full benefit of their origins, with their fresh fruit flavour and carefully integrated oak.

TASMANIA

Cooled by the Southern Ocean breezes, the vines of the Limestone Coast grow in a near perfect environment. The terra rossa soils of the area are influenced by the abundant deposits of limestone, that give the area its name. Reflecting the elements that created them, Ninth Island Limestone Coast shiraz, cabernet sauvignon and merlot are characterised by ripe, soft flavours and restrained, elegant structure.

LIMESTONE COAST

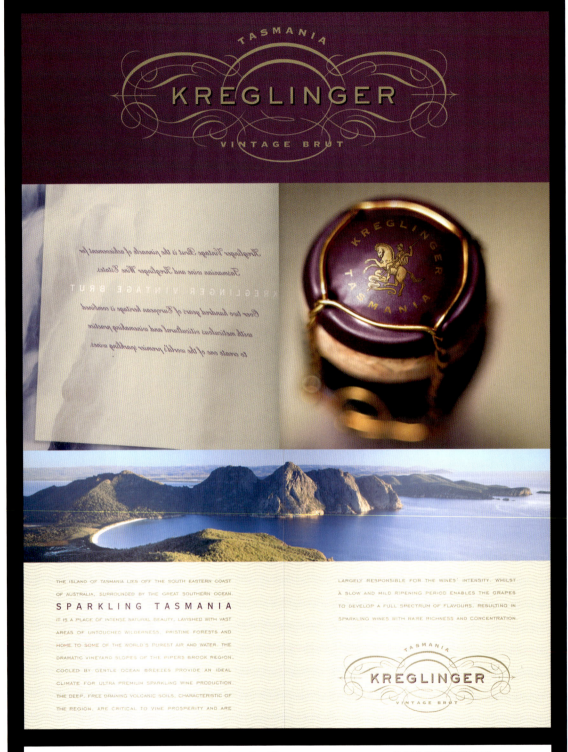

STUDIO
Harcus Design

CLIENT
Kreglinger

DESCRIPTION
Vintage brut

STUDIO	_CLIENT_	_DESCRIPTION_
Infinito Consultores	Infinito Consultores	Seafood products

STUDIO
Sayles Graphic Design

CLIENT
Knoxville Chamber of Commerce

DESCRIPTION
Exposition brochure

STUDIO	_CLIENT_	_DESCRIPTION_
Sayles Graphic Design	Knoxville Chamber of Commerce	Exposition brochure

["Larger sheets, such as those with detailed maps or expansive photo spreads, are folded into four, five, or six panels. Booklet brochures are made of multiple sheets most often saddle-stitched (stapled on the creased edge) or "perfect-bound" like a paperback book."]

STUDIO
Terminal 108

CLIENT
BMS

DESCRIPTION
Special environments

STUDIO	_CLIENT_	_DESCRIPTION_
Terminal 108	BMS	Special environments

STUDIO	_CLIENT_	_DESCRIPTION_
Terminal 108	BMS	Special environments

STUDIO	_CLIENT_	_DESCRIPTION_
Terminal 108	BMS	Special environments

STUDIO	_CLIENT_	_DESCRIPTION_
Bintang	Bintang	Street wear

STUDIO	_CLIENT_	_DESCRIPTION_
Magma Comunicação e Design	Backstage	Corporate brochure

STUDIO
Adriano Fidalgo

CLIENT
Cantão

DESCRIPTION
Fashion brand

STUDIO	_CLIENT_	_DESCRIPTION_
Redcafé Comunicação	Alligare	Floor in marble

STUDIO	_CLIENT_	_DESCRIPTION_
Verdes Campos	Samambaia	Printed material about art

STUDIO	_CLIENT_	_DESCRIPTION_
Amjad Olabi	Talulah New York	Form of luxury

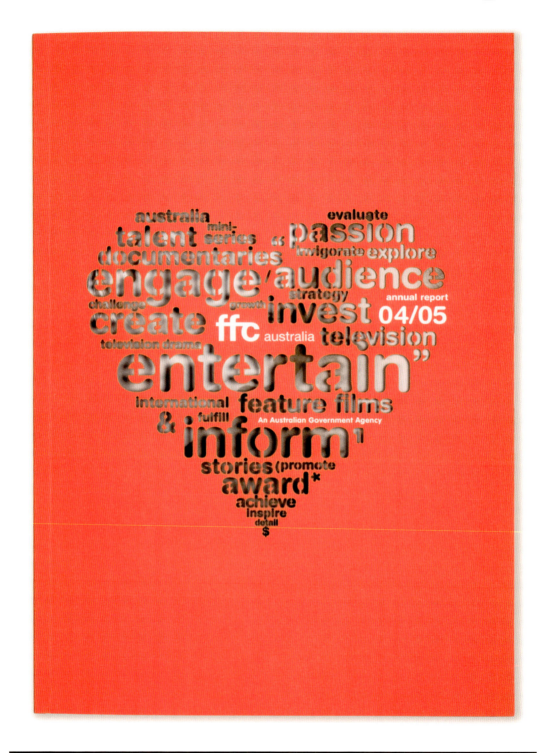

STUDIO	_CLIENT_	_DESCRIPTION_
Harcus Design	Harcus Design	Award achieve inspire

STUDIO	_CLIENT_	_DESCRIPTION_
Harcus Design	Harcus Design	Award achieve inspire

STUDIO
Hyperakt Design Group

CLIENT
Brooklyn C. of Commerce

DESCRIPTION
Annual report 06

STUDIO	_CLIENT_	_DESCRIPTION_
Hyperakt Design Group	Brooklyn C. of Commerce	Annual report 06

STUDIO
Hyperakt Design Group

CLIENT
Brooklyn C. of Commerce

DESCRIPTION
Annual report 06

STUDIO	_CLIENT_	_DESCRIPTION_
Hyperakt Design Group	Brooklyn C. of Commerce	Annual report 06

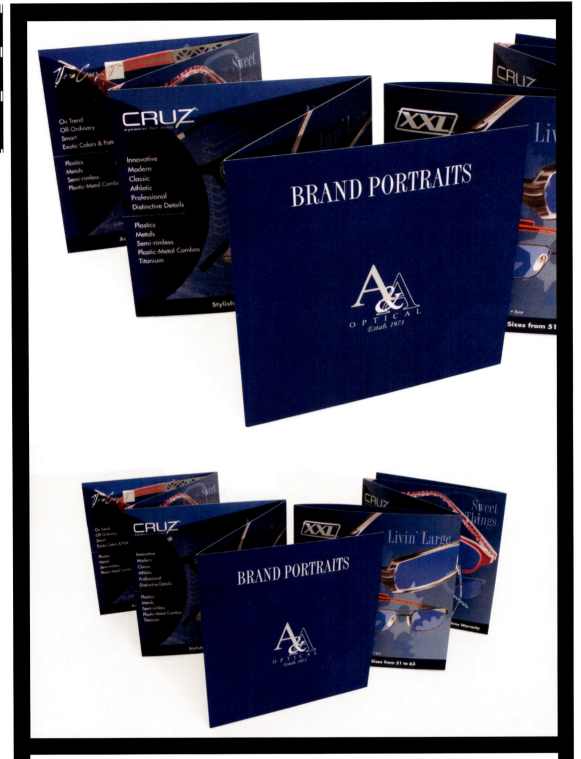

STUDIO
Jimmy Ball

CLIENT
A&A Optical

DESCRIPTION
Optical brand brochure

STUDIO	_CLIENT_	_DESCRIPTION_
Templin Brink Design	American Eagle	Fashion brand catalog

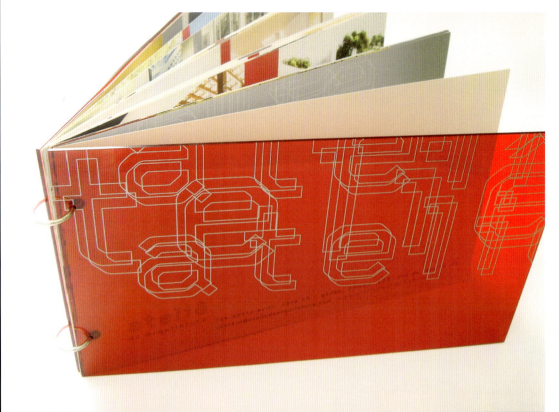

STUDIO	_CLIENT_	_DESCRIPTION_
Redondo Design	Ateliê de Arquitetura	Architecture office

STUDIO	_CLIENT_	_DESCRIPTION_
Redondo Design	CEG	Gas company

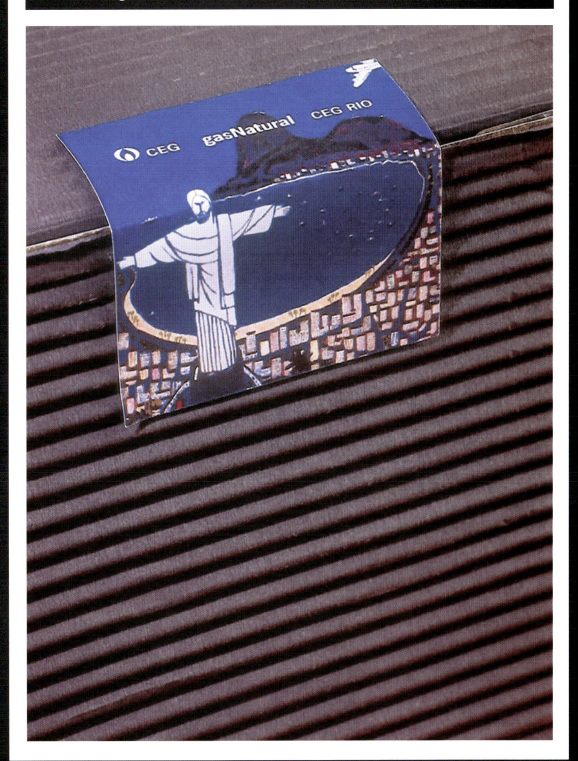

STUDIO	_CLIENT_	_DESCRIPTION_
Redondo Design	Confra Rio	Business Meeting

STUDIO	_CLIENT_	_DESCRIPTION_
Sebastiany Design	O Moteleiro	Motel guide

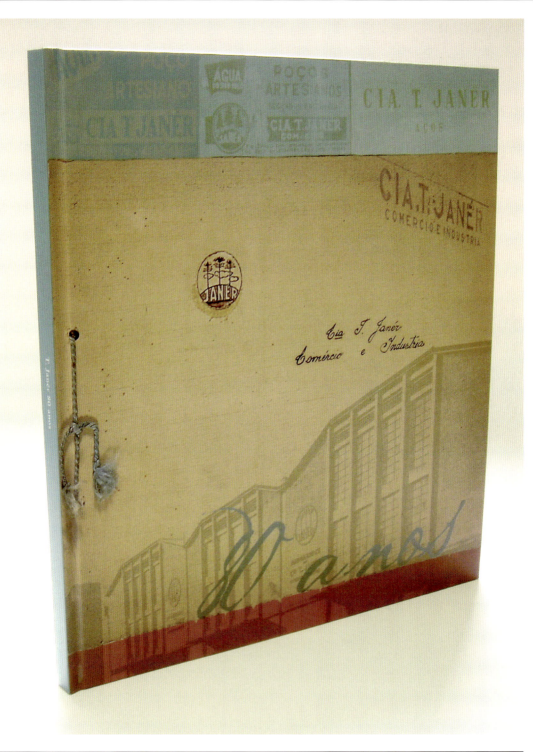

STUDIO	_CLIENT_	_DESCRIPTION_
Redondo Design	Jané	Steel industry

STUDIO	_CLIENT_	_DESCRIPTION_
Redondo Design	Jané	Steel industry

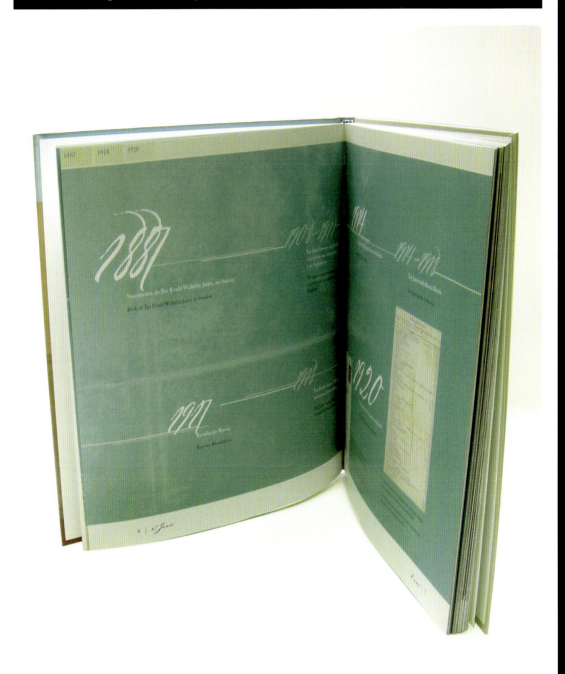

STUDIO	_CLIENT_	_DESCRIPTION_
Turnstyle	Steelcase	Annual report 06

STUDIO	_CLIENT_	_DESCRIPTION_
Turnstyle	Steelcase	Annual report 06

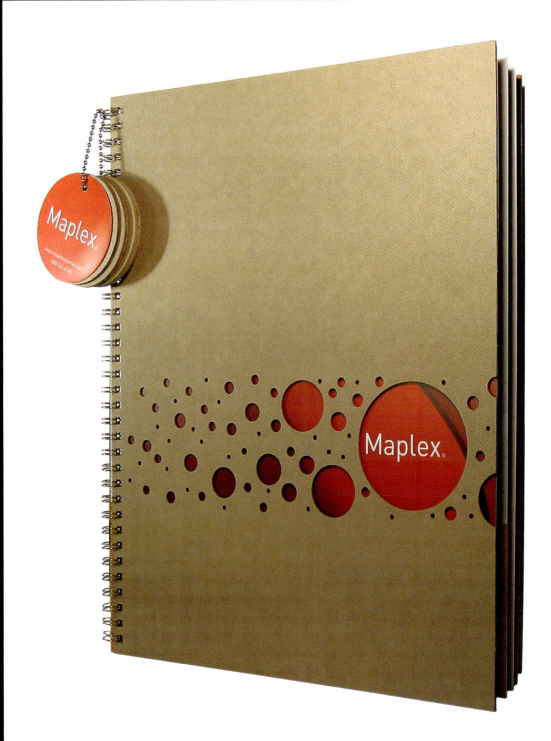

STUDIO	_CLIENT_	_DESCRIPTION_
MSLK	Maplex	Furniture

STUDIO
MSLK

CLIENT
Maplex

DESCRIPTION
Furniture

It's only natural

The Maplex brand is owned by Weidmann, a worldwide leader in fiber products manufacturing and engineering since 1877.

A dual-certified ISO 9001 and ISO 14001 company, Weidmann is committed to maintaining international quality and environmental management standards, and is proud to have been recognized as the first-ever "Vermont Business Environmental Leader" by the state's Agency of Natural Resources.

Maplex consists of 100% natural, unbleached wood fibers sourced from sustainably managed forests.

It's manufactured using nothing but water, pressure and heat.

No binders. No additives.

Nontoxic and entirely biodegradable, Maplex is safe for both people and the environment.

Consider it the future of fiberboard.

The perfect balance between strength and flexibility

A beautiful, sustainable alternative to wood, composites, metal and plastics, Maplex is both strong and bendable, making it an ideal material for interiors, furniture and consumer products.

Add one-of-a-kind details by cutting or stamping sheets with custom patterns, shapes or logos.

For the perfect finish, apply your choice of paints, stains, varnishes, waxes or veneers.

The shape of things to come

A dense but pliable matrix of softwood fibers, Maplex is more formable than wood, plywood or fiberboard.

Today, Maplex is turning up in all kinds of consumer products—from furniture to housewares and accessories. There's no telling what it might be used for next.

STUDIO	_CLIENT_	_DESCRIPTION_
Wing Chan Design	American Express	Business advice brochure

STUDIO	_CLIENT_	_DESCRIPTION_
Wing Chan Design	American Express	Business advice brochure

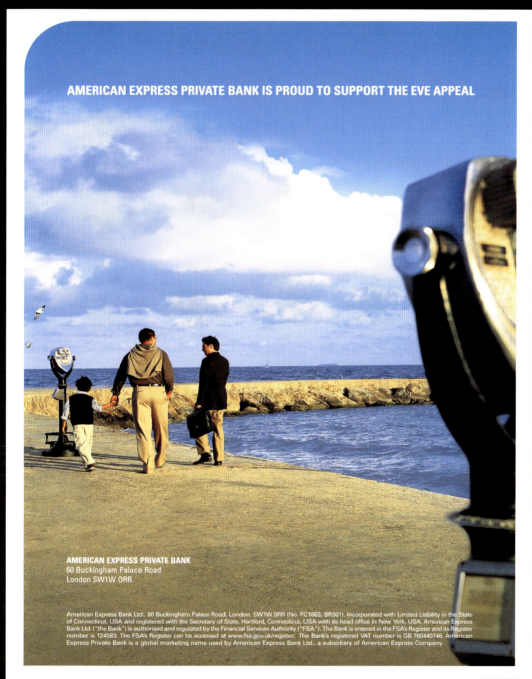

STUDIO
Wing Chan Design

CLIENT
American Express

DESCRIPTION
Business advice brochure

STUDIO	_CLIENT_	_DESCRIPTION_
Wing Chan Design	American Express	Product matrix brochure

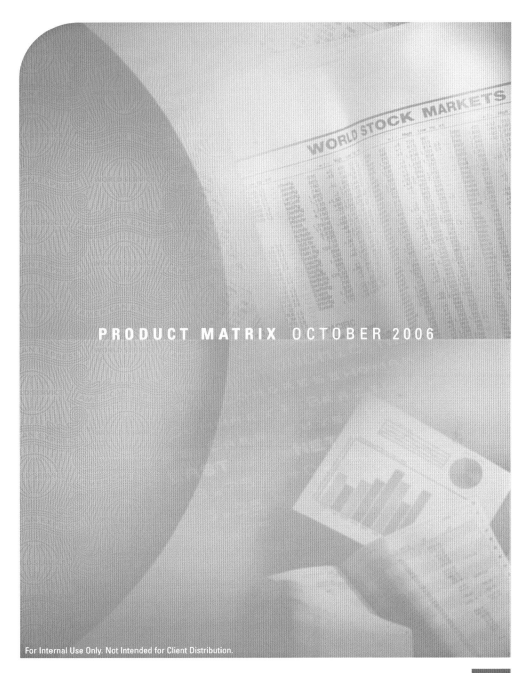

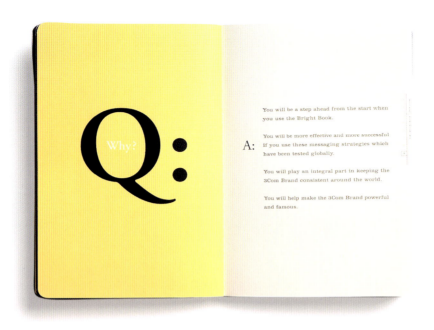

STUDIO	_CLIENT_	_DESCRIPTION_
Templin Brink Design	3Com	Brand character personality

STUDIO	_CLIENT_	_DESCRIPTION_
Templin Brink Design	3Com	Brand character personality

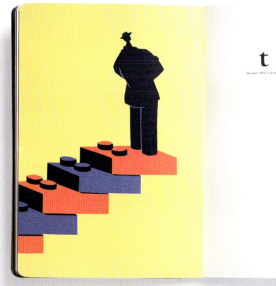

["Brochures are often printed using four-color process on thick gloss paper to give an initial impression of quality."]

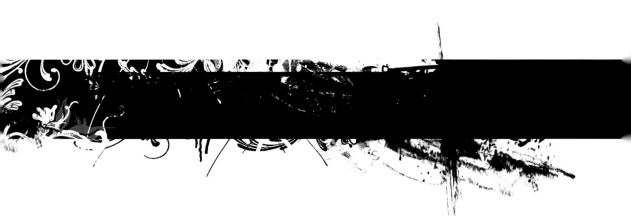

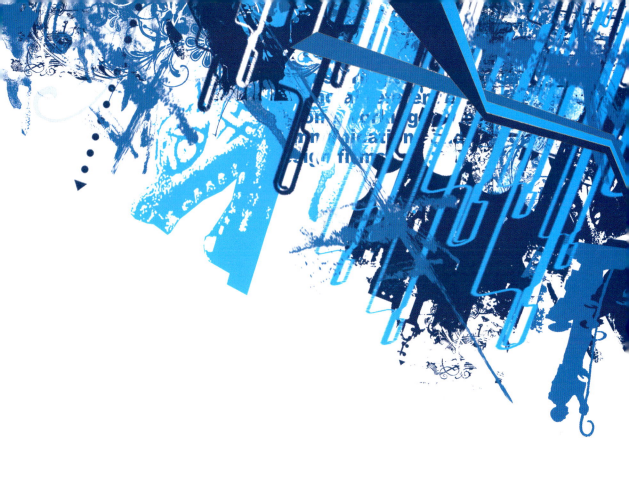

STUDIO	_CLIENT_	_DESCRIPTION_
Adriano Fidalgo	Helena Rubinstein	Cosmetic brochure

STUDIO	_CLIENT_	_DESCRIPTION_
Gouthier Design	Replenish	Laser treatments

STUDIO	_CLIENT_	_DESCRIPTION_
MSLK	Maybelline - New York	Cosmetic brands folder

STUDIO	_CLIENT_	_DESCRIPTION_
Red Circle Agency	Drug Free	Againt drug campaign

STUDIO	_CLIENT_	_DESCRIPTION_
Red Circle Agency	Drug Free	Againt drug campaign

METH Get the facts, learn the Science...

SOME SLANG NAMES INCLUDE:
Speed, Meth, Crystal, Crank, Chalk, Zip, Christy, Tina, Tweak, Flash, Fire, Go-fast, Ice, Glass, Uppers, or Quartz.

Methamphetamine affects your body:
- By creating a false sense of energy, meth pushes the body harder than it can safely handle
- Increased heart rate and blood pressure can lead to a stroke or heart attack
- Long-term use can cause uncontrolled shaking and tremors

Methamphetamine affects your self-control:
- Meth is a powerfully addictive drug
- Many users will become addicted after their first use
- Meth causes increased aggression, and violent or destructive behavior

- Depression
- Paranoia and extreme nervousness
- Seeing/hearing things that aren't there
- Permanent brain damage

Methamphetamine affects your appearance:
- Severe weight loss
- Dry and brittle hair
- Open sores or rashes
- Loss of teeth – "Meth mouth"

Methamphetamine changes your behavior:
- Dopamine - the brain chemical that makes us feel good - is released at above-normal levels when a person is using meth.
- Their brain is then tricked into thinking that it no longer needs to produce dopamine.
- The bottom line? Long-term use of meth, high dosages, or both can bring violent, aggressive behavior that's usually paired with extreme paranoia.

Methamphetamine kills.

Don't risk it...

Know the law.
Making, selling, and using methamphetamine is illegal in every state

Stay informed.
In 2004, meth use sent more people to the hospital emergency room than any other 'club' drug

Get the facts.
Meth is made from dangerous chemicals that are flammable, corrosive, and toxic. These chemicals can cause fires and explosions, and release toxic vapors that damage the environment and the health of meth makers and the people around them.

Know the risks using meth can cause:
- A severe "crash" after the first intense effects wear off
- Irreversible damage to blood vessels in your brain
- Long-term depression
- Bad health and unattractive appearance
- Risky behaviors leading to injury or disease, such as HIV or AIDS

RESOURCES

The Partnership for a Drug Free America

Information for this brochure was provided by The Partnership for a Drug-Free America, 2006. Used with permission.

For more information about methamphetamine, visit www.drugfree.org.

Additional Information can be found at:
www.methresources.gov
www.nometh.org
www.notevenonce.com
www.minnesotamethwatch.com
www.usdoj.gov/methawareness
www.ncai.org/Meth_in_Indian_Country_Initiat.192.0.html
www.health.state.mn.us/divs/eh/meth

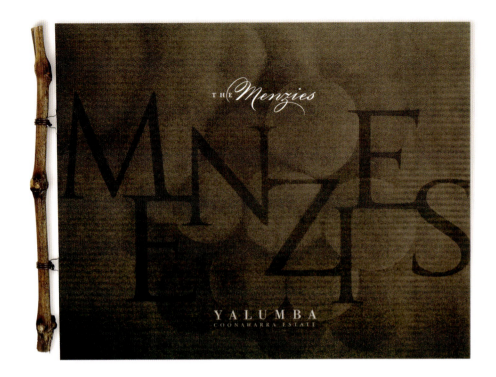

STUDIO	_CLIENT_	_DESCRIPTION_
Harcus Design	The Menzies	Yalumba estate presentation

STUDIO	_CLIENT_	_DESCRIPTION_
Wing Chan Design	ConXus	Biological laboratory

Campus Bay Business Park is a state of the art Research and Development Business Park with over 120,000 square feet of existing chemical and biological laboratory facilities and approvals for the development of an additional 360,000 square feet of laboratories and office space. Campus Bay Business Park is ideally located on Interstate Highway 580 along the San Francisco Bay. It is adjacent to the University of California, Berkeley Engineering Field Station and just ten minutes from the University of California, Berkeley main campus.

Ready to move in institutional quality laboratory space is fully equipped for scientific needs.

Amenities for employees include a shuttle to BART, showers, a sand volleyball court, outdoor patios and miles of recreation on the Bay Trail.

Six building campus with a variety of facilities offers a place for companies to develop and grow.

ConXus started with the questions: What if we bring skilled people and essential resources together with the aim of giving the best early stage companies a running start? Provide top flight laboratory and office space in a great location with a handful of emerging leaders in life sciences? Have company creation experts in close proximity with expertise in key areas of business planning, development and implementation? Offer seed level funding for those whose ideas merit it? What would happen when we connect these elements? We think great companies will emerge.

To meet this vision, **ConXus** has been formed by SIMEON Commercial Properties, Synexis cg, LLC, and SIMVEST. SIMEON is the developer of Campus Bay, a state of the art laboratory facility in Richmond, CA and many other life science research and development facilities located in key Bay Area clusters. Synexis CG is a national business services group that specializes in life science company creation and development. SIMVEST is a privately owned venture capital firm that provides seed financing for early stage life science companies.

ConXus
Campus Bay Business Park
4655 Meade Street
Richmond, CA 94804

ConXus

A Life Science Community   Campus Bay

ConXus
Campus Bay Business Park
4655 Meade Street
Richmond, CA 94804

www.conxus.com

ConXus

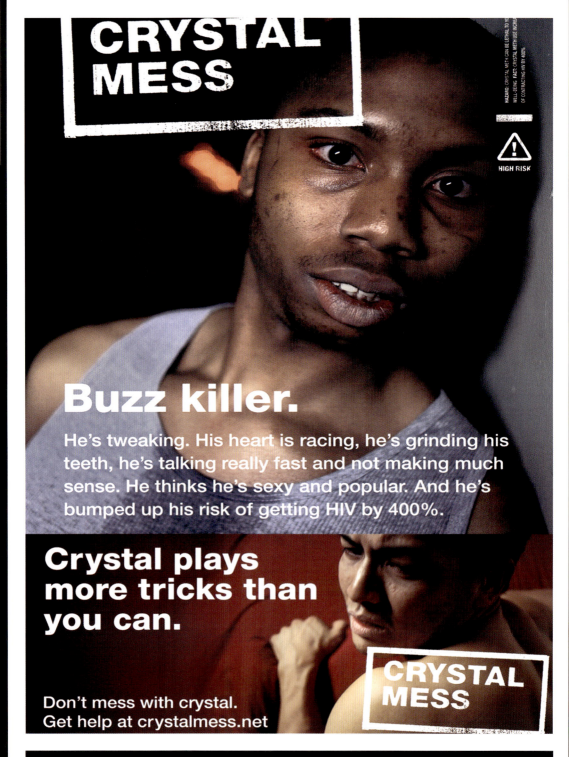

STUDIO	_CLIENT_	_DESCRIPTION_
Templin Brink Design	Crystal mess	High risk campaign

Your career took up too much time anyway.

A crystal meth habit can suck up your job, your friends, your home and your health in about 18 months. It's happened to lots of guys already. What a way to clear your schedule.

Don't mess with crystal.
Get help at crystalmess.net

CRYSTAL MESS

HAZARD: CRYSTAL METH CAN BE LETHAL TO YOUR HEALTH AND WELL-BEING. FACT: CRYSTAL METH USE INCREASES YOUR RISK OF CONTRACTING HIV BY 400%

HIGH RISK

STUDIO	_CLIENT_	_DESCRIPTION_
Segura-inc	Rock Shox	Accessories/technology for bikes

STUDIO	_CLIENT_	_DESCRIPTION_
Segura-inc	Rock Shox	Accessories/technology for bikes

STUDIO	_CLIENT_	_DESCRIPTION_
Segura-inc	Rock Shox	Accessories/technology for bikes

STUDIO	_CLIENT_	_DESCRIPTION_
Segura-inc	Rock Shox	Accessories/technology for bikes

STUDIO	_CLIENT_	_DESCRIPTION_
Segura-inc	Rock Shox	Accessories/technology for bikes

Healthcare
Biotechnology
Pharmaceuticals

NOONAN/RUSSO COMMUNICATIONS

STUDIO	_CLIENT_	_DESCRIPTION_
Wing Chan Design	NR Biotechnology	Corporate communications

STUDIO	_CLIENT_	_DESCRIPTION_
Wing Chan Design	NR Biotechnology	Corporate communications

VECTOR DEVELOPMENT

VECTORS: TRANSPORTING A GENE INTO A CELL

Today, the critical hurdle facing the widespread commercialization of gene therapies is the development of novel gene delivery vehicles or vectors. The vector used within a gene therapy construct determines the ability to deliver a gene to a specific tissue, cell or even a subcellular compartment, such as the nucleus, within the body. Once in the appropriate site, the gene can express its product at the desired level for the appropriate period of time. Because of the critical importance of vector development, RPR Gencell has invested heavily in the research and development of a broad portfolio of vectors.

THE ABILITY TO SELECT THE RIGHT VECTOR

Vector development is a highly competitive and evolving arena. Leading gene therapy researchers acknowledge that no single vector can deliver every gene to every target with the desired result. The key element establishing a gene therapy portfolio, therefore, is access to a variety of vector delivery systems and the ability to select the best vector delivery option for a specific disease. Through its network of collaborators, RPR Gencell has access to multiple existing vectors and advances in vector technology.

A variety of viral and non-viral vectors have been developed and tested, each providing a different mechanism of gene transfer with associated delivery profiles.

VIRAL VECTORS

Currently, the most efficient and commonly used vectors for gene therapy are "defective" or nonreplicating viral vectors. While RPR Gencell and its network partners are developing expertise in many classes of viral vectors, such as retroviruses, adeno-associated viruses and herpes-simplex viruses, the current clinical programs utilize adenovirus vectors. The adenovirus is a human virus to which the general population has commonly been exposed and which does not cause human disease. Adenoviruses have several advantages, including:

- ability to infect both dividing and non-dividing cells
- high efficiency of gene transfer
- high levels of gene expression
- no integration into the host genome
- ability to be produced in very high quantities

The ability of the adenovirus vector to deliver and express a p53 gene inside a cell was validated in the clinic by Dr. Jack Roth of M. D. Anderson Cancer Center,

an RPR Gencell collaborator via Introgen Therapeutics. Dr. Roth and his colleagues demonstrated that the p53/adenoviral construct could be delivered via injection directly into tumor cells and express the p53 protein, thus inducing apoptosis, or programmed cell death, in many of the treated tumors. Additionally, no significant adverse side effects were observed associated with the adenovirus vector.

RPR Gencell is conducting a major effort internally and through its collaborators, mainly with Dr. Michel Perricaudet, Director of Research of the Centre National de la Recherche Scientifique (CNRS) at the Institut Gustave Roussy, to develop second- and third-generation adenovirus vectors.

NON-VIRAL VECTORS

Parallel to its development of viral vectors, RPR Gencell is also strongly committed to non-viral vector research, which when optimized will take a significant place in gene delivery.

In collaboration with the CNRS, RPR Gencell has created a joint research unit staffed by 29 researchers dedicated to non-viral vector development and improved formulations. In addition to the development of novel chemical vectors, efforts to improve DNA packaging techniques and to engineer novel plasmid constructs are ongoing. As chemical vectors will play an increasingly important role in gene delivery, RPR Gencell has also established a collaboration in this field with the laboratory of Nobel prize-winning chemist Jean-Marie Lehn.

RPR Gencell is also working with network partners on the development of single-chain antibodies as DNA delivery vehicles. Single-chain antibodies recognize specific molecules within the body and therefore can be utilized to deliver a specific gene to an intended target

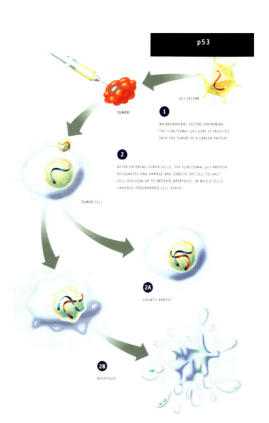

STUDIO	_CLIENT_	_DESCRIPTION_
Sayles Graphic Design	Mid-Iowa	Health Foundation

STUDIO	_CLIENT_	_DESCRIPTION_
Sayles Graphic Design	Mid-Iowa	Health Foundation

STUDIO
Savio Alphonso

CLIENT
California State University

DESCRIPTION
Magazine and brochure about sleep

STUDIO	_CLIENT_	_DESCRIPTION_
Savio Alphonso	California State University	Magazine and brochure about sleep

["Businesses may turn out small quantities of brochures on a computer printer, but offset printing turns out higher quantities for less cost."]

STUDIO	_CLIENT_	_DESCRIPTION_
Gouthier Design	The Dub House	Interactive CD + brochure

STUDIO	_CLIENT_	_DESCRIPTION_
Gouthier Design	The Dub House	Interactive CD + brochure

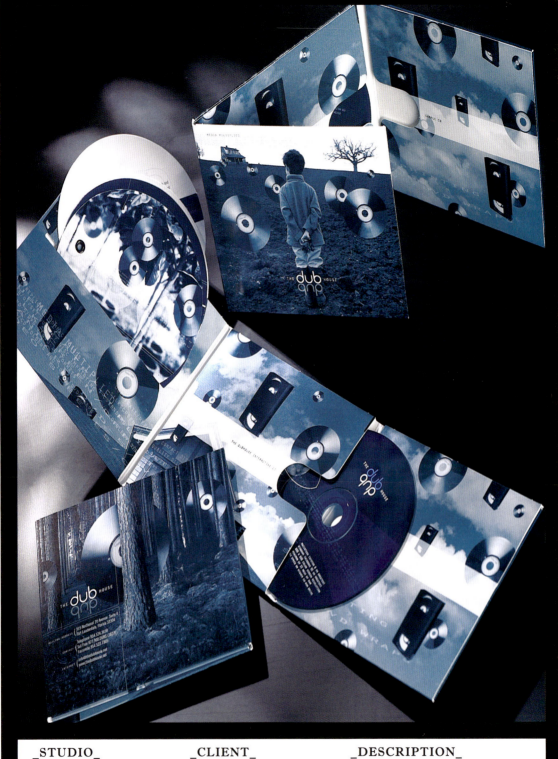

STUDIO	_CLIENT_	_DESCRIPTION_
Gouthier Design	The Dub House	Interactive CD + brochure

STUDIO	_CLIENT_	_DESCRIPTION_
Gouthier Design	The Dub House	Interactive CD + brochure

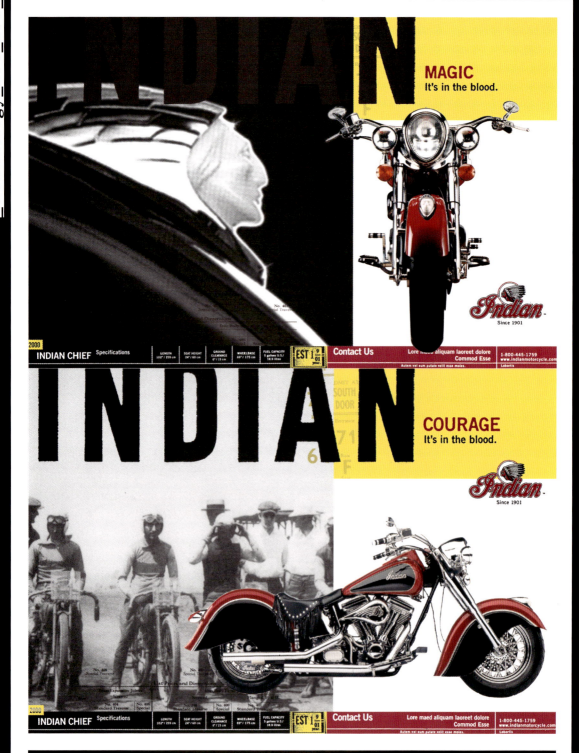

If you want to make it big,

MAKE IT BIG

This sturdy light-weight portable display has been designed with ease-of-use in mind and comes with brilliant, high-quality printing!

High impact that lasts!
Printed on Anvy's non-curl Fari fabric with ink guaranteed to maintain its vibrancy for up to 5 years, Anvy's high-resolution, full-colour banner graphics are bold and beautifully clear.

Five-Year Guarantee!
The banner stand's durable metal construction protects your graphics during transport. We provide a 5-year guarantee against hardware defects.

Not just for trade shows.
These high-impact banner stands are perfect for all point-of-presence locations: restaurants, businesses, lobbies – anywhere you want to get noticed with a professional, high-quality display.

Easy to use.
Banner stands are quick, safe and easy for one person to set up and take down.

Flexible.
Want to change your message from time to time? Easy: just contact us to print new art for your banner stand.

only **$479.00**
MSRP $839.95

Mention our special promotion code [**2244**] when ordering to receive this special pricing.

Order now – offer may expire without notice.

Completion is 3-10 days from receipt of art.

Price includes one Prestige banner stand, high-resolution full-colour digital printing of your graphic design, custom carry bag and assembly of banner stand. Visual image size is 33.5" wide x 81" tall. Artwork to be supplied in ready-to-print format. Contact Anvy Digital Imaging for specs or to request design services.

Anvy Digital Imaging prints all large format items, including: vehicle wrap graphics, decals, trade show displays, large posters, see-through window decals and much more.

Anvy Digital Imaging   #6, 3610 29 Street N.E., Calgary, Alberta T1Y-5Z7   T: (403) **291-2244**   F: (403) 291-2246

STUDIO	_CLIENT_	_DESCRIPTION_
Randy Milanovic MGDC	Anvy	Digital Imaging

STUDIO	_CLIENT_	_DESCRIPTION_
Ivan Blanco Lorenzo	Yamaha	Motor sport

STUDIO	_CLIENT_	_DESCRIPTION_
Harcus Design	Got it!	Digital Asset Management

STUDIO	_CLIENT_	_DESCRIPTION_
Harcus Design	Got it!	Digital Asset Management

STUDIO	_CLIENT_	_DESCRIPTION_
3rd Edge Communications	Feration	Software management folder

STUDIO	_CLIENT_	_DESCRIPTION_
Magma Comunicação e Design	Transpetro	Corporate brand brochure

STUDIO	_CLIENT_	_DESCRIPTION_
Templin Brink Design	Delta-Air	Airline industry

STUDIO	_CLIENT_	_DESCRIPTION_
Templin Brink Design	Delta-Air	Airline industry

> "Compared with a flyer or handbill, a brochure usually uses higher-quality paper, more color, and is folded."

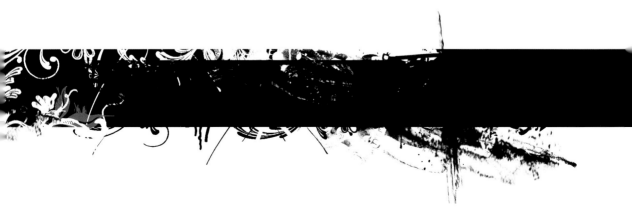

STUDIO	_CLIENT_	_DESCRIPTION_
Oliver Kuy	Nike	World cup celebration

STUDIO	_CLIENT_	_DESCRIPTION_
Templin Brink Design	Oakland	Heckling lessons

TAKE ★ HECKLING ★ LESSONS

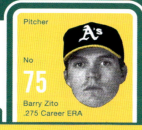

ZITO IS NEATO

SUPPORT YOUR 2003 Season

STUDIO
Hybrid Design

CLIENT
Nike

DESCRIPTION
Running Summit Press Kit

STUDIO	_CLIENT_	_DESCRIPTION_
Hybrid Design	Nike	Running Summit Press Kit

STUDIO
Hybrid Design

CLIENT
Nike

DESCRIPTION
Corporate Responsibility Report

STUDIO
Hybrid Design

CLIENT
Nike

DESCRIPTION
Corporate Responsibility Report

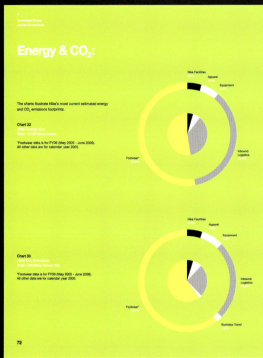

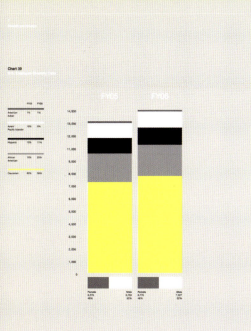

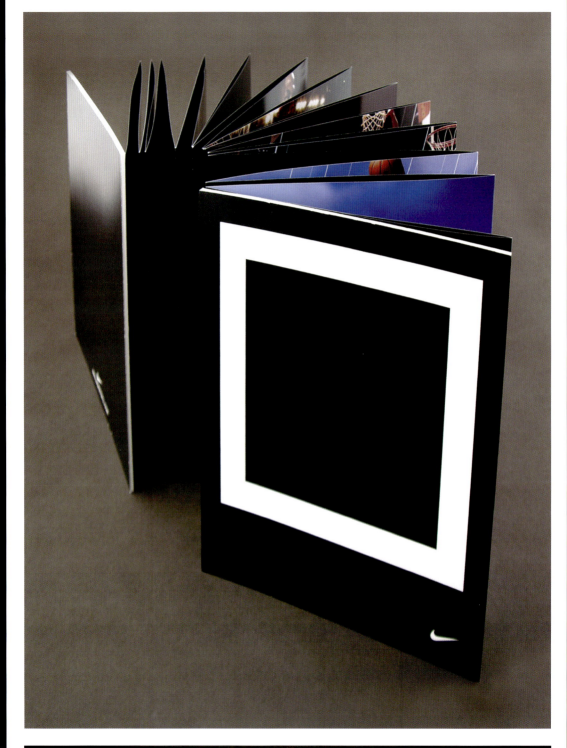

STUDIO	_CLIENT_	_DESCRIPTION_
Hybrid Design	Nike	Basketball event Press kit

STUDIO	_CLIENT_	_DESCRIPTION_
Hybrid Design	Nike	Basketball event Press kit

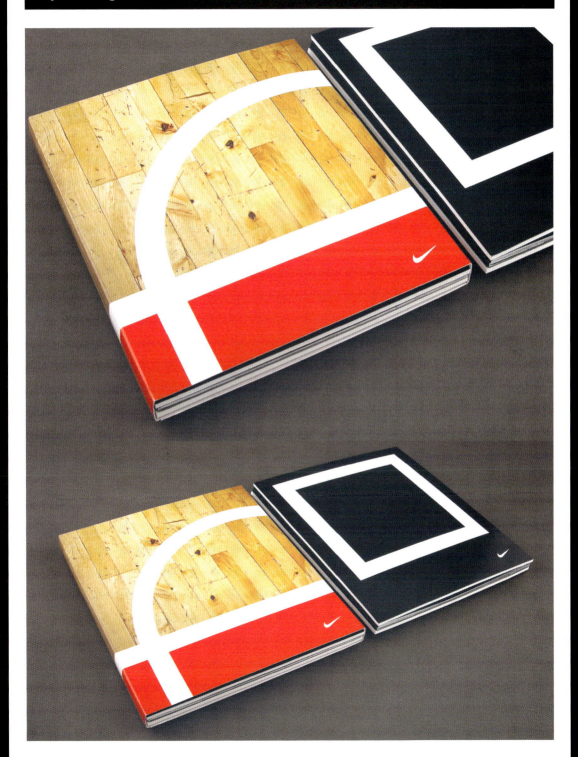

STUDIO	_CLIENT_	_DESCRIPTION_
Hybrid Design	Nike	Triumphant moments

| _STUDIO_ | _CLIENT_ | _DESCRIPTION_ |
| Hybrid Design | Nike | Triumphant moments |

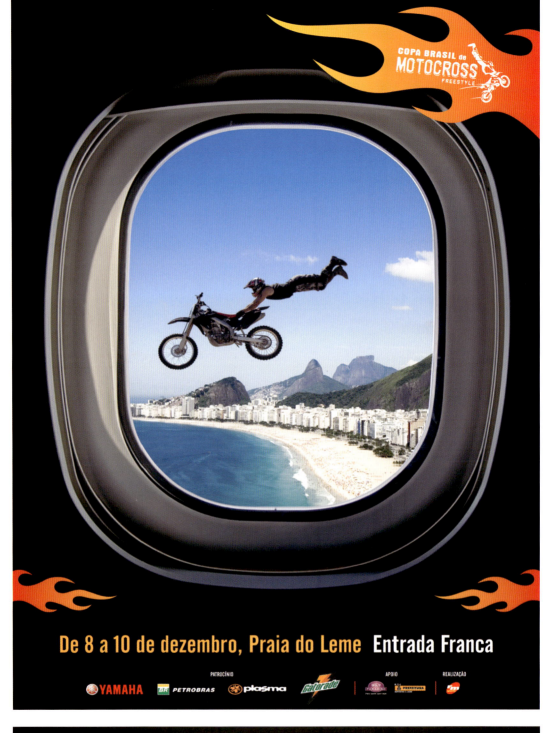

STUDIO	_CLIENT_	_DESCRIPTION_
Camisa 10	Petrobras	Surf event

STUDIO	_CLIENT_	_DESCRIPTION_
Sockeye Creative	La Prima	Atlanta Adidas 2002

STUDIO	_CLIENT_	_DESCRIPTION_
Sockeye Creative	New Orleans Louisiana	Sole of Adidas 2003

STUDIO
Turnstyle

CLIENT
Reebok

DESCRIPTION
Women´s athletic shoes

STUDIO	_CLIENT_	_DESCRIPTION_
Turnstyle	Reebok	Women's athletic shoes

STUDIO
MSLK

CLIENT
Tom Welling

DESCRIPTION
Sport presentation

STUDIO	_CLIENT_	_DESCRIPTION_
MSLK	Tom Welling	Sport presentation

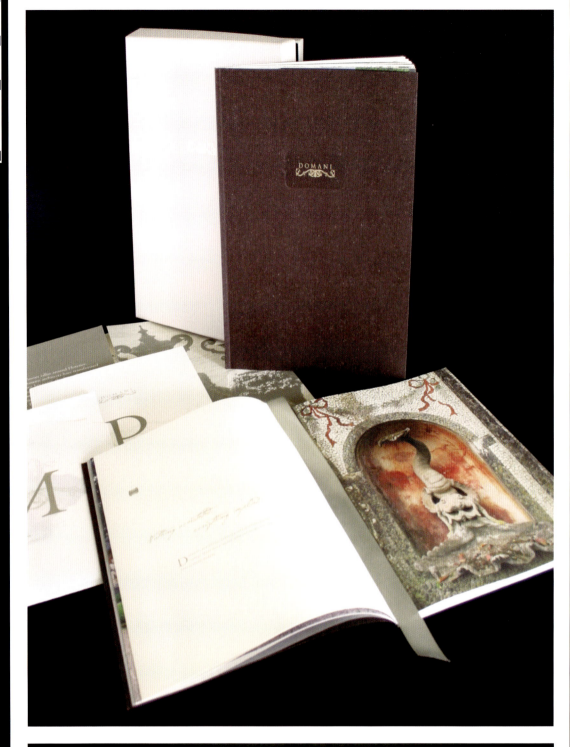

STUDIO	_CLIENT_	_DESCRIPTION_
Gouthier Design	Domani	Architecture office

INTRODUÇÃO

Este livro relata, contextualiza e analisa a experiência da Fundação de Defesa dos Direitos Humanos Bento Rubião em torno do direito à moradia. É o primeiro de dois volumes a serem editados com o apoio da *Building Social Housing Foundation – BSHF*, sediada na Inglaterra. Neste primeiro volume aborda-se o trabalho de assessoria a grupos populares, desenvolvido na região metropolitana do Rio de Janeiro, visando seu acesso, a permanência e a regularização jurídica da terra urbana que ocupam.

O projeto institucional que trata desta questão, denominado *Projeto Direito à Terra*, é a atividade original da Fundação, criada em 1986. Grupos de técnicos e lideranças de comunidades faveladas, trouxeram a experiência nesta temática desenvolvida por anos na *Pastoral de Favelas da Arquidiocese do Rio de Janeiro*.

A questão da terra urbana no Brasil é um emaranhado de fios, exatamente como mostra a capa desta publicação, ao retratar um poste de distribuição de energia elétrica na favela da Rocinha, no Rio de Janeiro. As razões para tal emaranhado, o mesmo acontecendo com a questão fundiária, são muitas, assim como suas consequências.

O *Projeto Direito à Terra*, com 20 anos de experiência, quer contribuir na busca de soluções para esta questão, permitindo à população pobre de cidades como o Rio de Janeiro o usufruto de um direito humano básico: um chão para morar com segurança.

INTRODUCTION

This book describes, contextualises and analyses the experience of the Fundação de Defesa dos Direitos Humanos Bento Rubião (Bento Rubião Foundation) in relation to the right to land. It is the first of two volumes to be published with the support of the Building and Social Housing Foundation (BSHF), based in the United Kingdom. This first volume addresses the work of the Bento Rubião Foundation in assisting low-income groups in the metropolitan area of Rio de Janeiro, to gain access, permanence and regularisation of the urban land that they occupy.

The institutional project that deals with this issue, the Right to Land Project, dates back to the origins of the Foundation, which was established in 1986. Groups of technical experts and leaders of informal settlements (favelas) brought their experience of this issue, developed over years in the Pastoral de Favelas (Slum Commission) of the Archdiocese of Rio de Janeiro.

The issue of urban land in Brazil is like a cluster of tangled wires, as shown on the cover of this publication with the image of an electrical post in the favela of Rocinha, in Rio de Janeiro. The reasons for this entanglement, just as with the land issue, are many, as are the consequences.

The Right to Land Project, with 20 years of experience, seeks to contribute to the search for solutions to this issue, enabling the poor in cities such as Rio de Janeiro to exercise and enjoy a basic human right: a place to live in safety.

STUDIO	_CLIENT_	_DESCRIPTION_
Ana Soares	Bento Rubião	Land and housing rights

STUDIO	_CLIENT_	_DESCRIPTION_
Ana Soares	Bento Rubião	Land and housing rights

STUDIO	_CLIENT_	_DESCRIPTION_
Dmyk	PA	Animal ilustration

STUDIO	_CLIENT_	_DESCRIPTION_
Dmyk	PA	Animal ilustration

STUDIO	_CLIENT_	_DESCRIPTION_
Dmyk	Finstral	Graphic design essays

STUDIO	_CLIENT_	_DESCRIPTION_
Dmyk	Finstral	Graphic design essays

STUDIO	_CLIENT_	_DESCRIPTION_
Sockeye Creative	Portland Opera	Opera season catalog

STUDIO
Randy Milanovic MGDC

CLIENT
Mash Project

DESCRIPTION
Againt domestic abuse

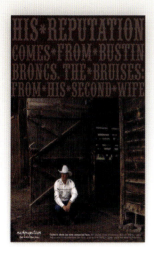
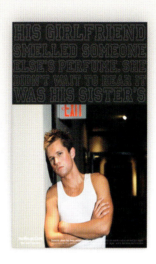
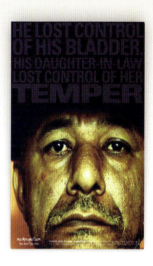

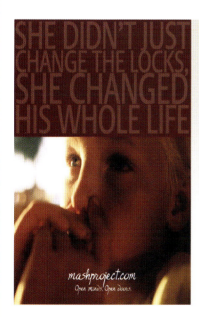

Mens Alternative Safe House – MASHproject

Domestic abuse has many unexpected faces. Men and their children also experience abuse and need your support. Help us create the Mens Alternative Safe House - a safe space for healing in Calgary – and let them know they're not alone.

We are working towards providing men and fathers with children an opportunity to remove themselves from a potentially explosive domestic situation. The fulfillment of our goal to provide beds for these people in need is imminent.

Show your support – help us raise the funds required to open our first home by purchasing these awareness posters today.

Visit us online at www.mashproject.com to place your order (8.5"x11" $25 ea, 24"x32" $100 ea CDN)

Posters designed by HandyRandy Communications Inc.

All profits go to this MASHproject initiative.

MASHproject.com is an initiative in support of the Family of Men Support Society, a peer support organization based in Calgary, Alberta, Canada.

mashproject.com
Open minds. Open doors.

STUDIO
Templin Brink Design

CLIENT
Target Stores

DESCRIPTION
Art that work

STUDIO	_CLIENT_	_DESCRIPTION_
Templin Brink Design	Target Stores	Art that work

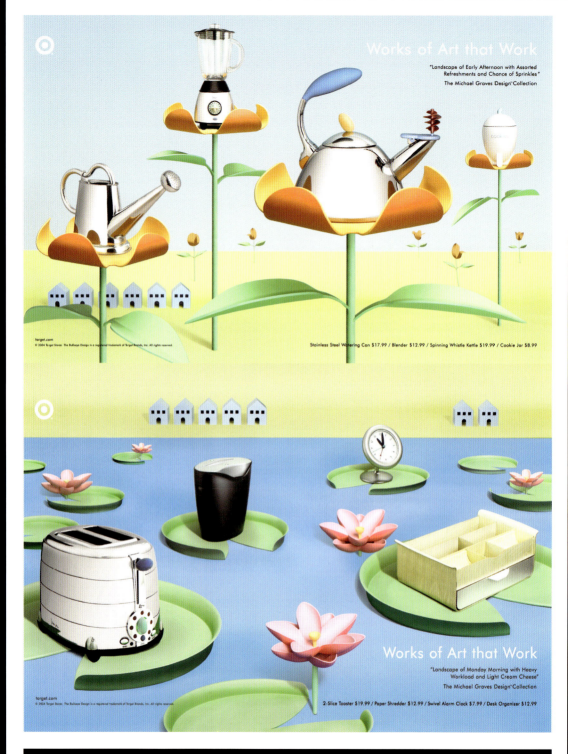

STUDIO	_CLIENT_	_DESCRIPTION_
Templin Brink Design	Target Stores	Art that work

STUDIO	_CLIENT_	_DESCRIPTION_
Templin Brink Design	Target Stores	Art that work

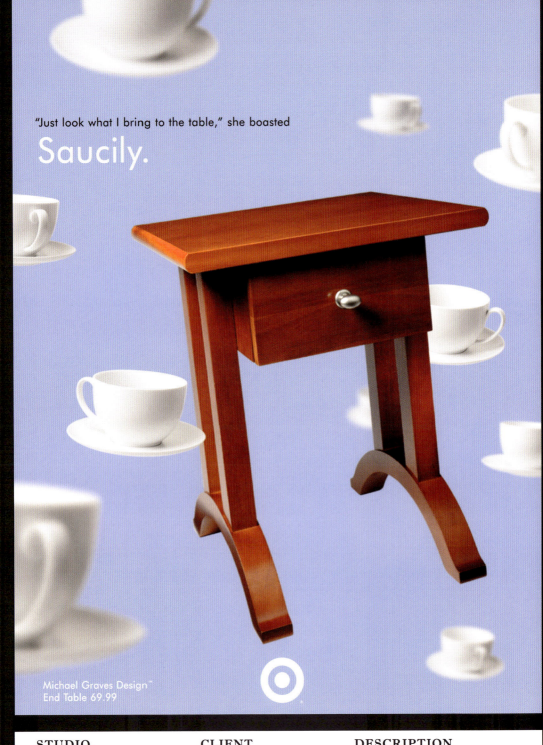

STUDIO	_CLIENT_	_DESCRIPTION_
Templin Brink Design	Target Stores	Art that work

STUDIO	_CLIENT_	_DESCRIPTION_
Templin Brink Design	Target Stores	Art that work

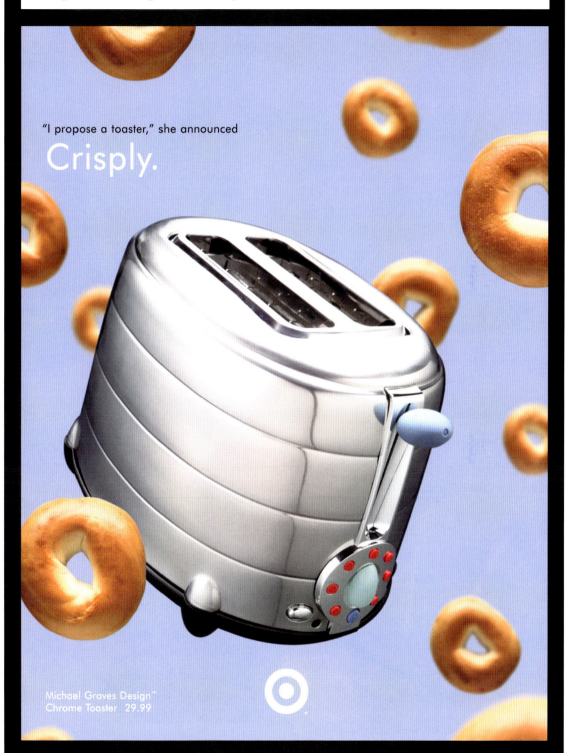

"I propose a toaster," she announced
Crisply.

Michael Graves Design™
Chrome Toaster 29.99

STUDIO	_CLIENT_	_DESCRIPTION_
Arte & Parte/Omnilife	Butacas Club Chivas	Mexican soccer club

STUDIO	_CLIENT_	_DESCRIPTION_
Arte & Parte/Omnilife	Butacas Club Chivas	Mexican soccer club

INDUSTRY

Officially incorporated in 1892, Franklin Park sprouted up from the intersection of the Midwest's largest freight lines and continues to serve as one of Chicagoland's most active rail hubs.

Accessibility and a hearty Midwest work ethic ensured Franklin Park's success and expansion, making it the ideal location for countless American headquarters over the years: World War II brought Douglas Aircraft and Buick Motors while the post-war economy attracted many technology-focused companies including Motorola.

1 | jdl.

MOTOROLA

In fact, The Grand Lofts building was originally a Motorola manufacturing center that produced some of the country's most advanced televisions, radios and phonographs. The building itself was a technical marvel of its time. It offered air-conditioned, "music-while-you-work" environments for its assembly line workers, an executive car lift that delivered the president's automobile directly to his office and a helicopter landing pad for traffic-free travel between the airport and the plant's Augusta Boulevard factory.

COMPLETED 1960 • $7,000,000 • 327,000 SQ FT • ENOUGH POWER TO LIGHT EVERY HOME IN FRANKLIN PARK • 2.5 MILES OF OFFICE PARTITIONS • 1,850 TONS OF AIR CONDITIONING DUCTS THAT COULD STRETCH FROM CHICAGO TO ROCKFORD • 5 MILES OF DUCT FOR TELEPHONE AND TELEGRAPH WIRING • 1,600,000 BRICKS • 10 MILES OF 5 FT LONG FLUORESCENT FIXTURES • A HUGE DIESEL GENERATOR FOR POWER FAILURES • A HELIPAD WITH A BELL 47H1 HELICOPTER CAPABLE OF 90 MPH • AN ESCALATOR RUNNING FROM THE FIRST TO FIFTH FLOORS MOVING AT 90 FEET PER MINUTE GOING UP AND 120 FEET PER MINUTE GOING DOWN • 2 PASSENGER ELEVATORS, 1 FREIGHT ELEVATOR, 1 FOOD LIFT AND A CAR ELEVATOR DIRECT TO THE PRESIDENT'S OFFICE

 COLOR TV!

jdl. | 2

STUDIO	_CLIENT_	_DESCRIPTION_
Firebelly Design	JDL Development	Grand Lofts brochure

STUDIO	_CLIENT_	_DESCRIPTION_
Firebelly Design	JDL Development	Grand Lofts brochure

DIRECTORY

3rd Edge Communications - 028, 138, 139, 140, 141, 280

Adriano Fidalgo - 072, 214, 244

Amjad Olabi - 217

Ana Soares - 305, 306, 307

Archrival - 036, 037, 134, 135, 136, 137

Arte & Parte/Omnilife - 320, 321

BBK Studio - 080, 081, 082, 083, 084, 085

Bintang - 212

Blok Design - 088, 089, 090

Boompje Studios - 144

Camisa 10 - 246, 296, 297

Charlotte Noruzi - 032, 033

Delrancho - 116, 117

Dmyk - 308, 309, 310, 311

Evio Design - 076, 077, 078, 079

Firebelly Design - 322, 323

Gouthier Design - 014, 015, 064, 065, 066, 067, 068, 069, 070, 071, 142, 245, 270, 271, 272, 273, 304

Guerrilha CT - 170, 171

Harcus Design - 198, 199, 200, 201, 202, 218, 219, 250, 278, 279

Hybrid Design - 182, 183, 288, 289, 290, 291, 292, 293, 294, 295

Hyperakt Design Group - 010, 011, 012, 013, 034, 035, 153, 154, 155, 156, 157, 158, 159, 160, 161, 162, 163, 164, 165, 166, 167, 190, 191, 220, 221, 222, 223

Ida Cheinman - 016, 017, 018, 019, 074, 078, 079

Infinito Consultores - 203

Ivan Blanco Lorenzo - 026, 277

Jimmy Ball - 224

Jose Luis Guerrero Garcia - 039

Julien Vallée - 100, 101

Karim Zariffa - 060, 061, 110, 111, 112, 113, 114, 115

Laranja Design - 172

Laura Varsky - 020, 021, 022, 023, 143

Magma Comunicação e Design - 030, 031, 038, 213, 281

Mario Fuentes - 194, 195, 196, 197

Mary Hutchison - 254, 255

Matrix - Breno Carvalho - 146

Miki Guadamur - 151

Mid west is best - 184, 185

MSLK - 073, 091, 234, 235, 247, 302, 303

Mujica TMP - 150

Nicola Place - 086, 087

Oliver Kuy - 286

Randy Milanovic MGDC - 152, 276, 313

Redcafé Comunicação - 192, 215

Red Circle Agency - 248, 249

Redondo Design - 040, 041, 226, 227, 228, 230, 231

Rodrigo Maciel Lima Marins - 042, 043, 044, 148

Sagmeister Inc - 027, 029, 102, 103, 104, 105, 106, 107, 108, 109, 173, 174, 175, 176, 177, 178, 179

Sangre.tv - 145, 147, 149, 180, 181

Savio Alphonso - 128, 129, 266, 267

Sayles Graphic Design - 075, 130, 131, 204, 205, 264, 265

Sebastiany Design - 045, 229

Segura-inc - 256, 257, 258, 259, 260, 261

Sifon - 118, 119, 120, 121, 122, 123

Sockeye Creative - 046, 047, 048, 049, 050, 051, 052, 054, 055, 169, 298, 299, 312

Templin Brink Design - 056, 057, 096, 097, 098, 099, 225, 240, 241, 252, 253, 274, 275, 282, 283, 287, 314, 315, 316, 317, 318, 319

Terminal 108 - 208, 209, 210, 211

Turnstyle - 058, 059, 092, 093, 094, 095, 232, 233, 300, 301

Unmarked Vehicle - 024, 025, 188, 189

Valeria Prada - 168

Verdes Campos - 216

Veronica Ettedgui - 193

Wing Chan Design - 053, 236, 237, 238, 239, 251, 262, 263

Wonksite Studio - 124, 125, 126, 127

AUTHOR

THANKS

www.mitodesign.com
-
To all my friends / students / clients
HAVE A NICE DAY!!!